"Based on her years of experience, Carol Kent has given us a book of rich insight and practical advice about public speaking. If you plan to teach a group of five or 50,000, read this book. These principles really work."

—LUCI SWINDOLL, Women of Faith speaker; author;
vice president of public relations, Insight for Living

"*Speak Up with Confidence* is a must-read for people who are committed to Christ and want to communicate their faith with greater impact. I've attended several Speak Up workshops and continue to learn fresh approaches to enhance my writing, speaking, business, and ministry leadership."

—KATHE WUNNENBERG, speaker;
author of *Grieving the Loss of a Loved One*

"What a joy to read a how-to book that really addresses the how-to. Carol Kent has systematically covered the details that have made her an outstanding speaker. I am delighted to recommend this book to the throngs of people who yearn to speak up with confidence."

—JEANNETTE CLIFT GEORGE, founder and artistic director,
A.D. Players, a Christian Drama Company; writer; public speaker

"You will not find a more excellent communicator than Carol Kent. When I hear her speak, I listen in rapt attention, and while reading her book, I could not put it down. In *Speak Up with Confidence*, she unselfishly shares her effective secrets with us. This is must reading whether you are a beginner or have been speaking for years."

—NEY BAIELY, author and international speaker

"Going into a seminar led by Carol Kent is like walking into a highly charged magnetic field. It is exciting! Things are popping, and you have to keep moving! It is more than energy and enthusiasm; it is a deep-rooted faith in God as revealed in Jesus Christ."

—DR. NELL MAHONEY, author and speaker

"When Carol Kent speaks, people listen! She is a highly trained, energetic, and gifted woman. Her insight and understanding of people, as well as her ability to communicate God's truth, make her one of the leaders in the Christian women's world."

— PAUL MATTHEWS, Tuscon, Arizona

WHAT SPEAK UP SEMINAR PARTICIPANTS ARE SAYING

"I would recommend the Speak Up with Confidence seminar to anyone desiring to share his or her faith with one person or a thousand."

— PAT PROBASCO, Speak Up seminar participant

"I would recommend this workshop to everyone. Who would not benefit from learning how to better represent themselves, their organization, or the Lord?"

— THEA RILEY, Speak Up seminar participant

"I was so blessed with the Speak Up conference. I increased my learning abundantly and it was fun, too. I have a BA in Bible theology and taught in a Bible college for fifteen years, and presenting this kind of talk is quite different but is something I always wanted to do."

— MARTHA HARTMAN, Speak Up seminar participant

Speak Up

WITH

Confidence

A STEP-BY-STEP GUIDE FOR SPEAKERS AND LEADERS

Revised and Updated Edition

Carol Kent

NAVPRESS

NAVPRESS⬤

NavPress is the publishing ministry of The Navigators, an international Christian organization and leader in personal spiritual development. NavPress is committed to helping people grow spiritually and enjoy lives of meaning and hope through personal and group resources that are biblically rooted, culturally relevant, and highly practical.

**For a free catalog go to www.NavPress.com
or call 1.800.366.7788 in the United States or 1.800.839.4769 in Canada.**

© 1997, 2007 by Carol Kent

All rights reserved. No part of this publication may be reproduced in any form without written permission from NavPress, P.O. Box 35001, Colorado Springs, CO 80935. www.navpress.com

NAVPRESS and the NAVPRESS logo are registered trademarks of NavPress. Absence of ® in connection with marks of NavPress or other parties does not indicate an absence of registration of those marks.

ISBN-13: 978-1-60006-144-8

Cover design by Arvid Wallen
Cover photo by Don Jones Photography

Some of the anecdotal illustrations in this book are true to life and are included with the permission of the persons involved. All other illustrations are composites of real situations, and any resemblance to people living or dead is coincidental.

(Originally published as *Speak Up with Confidence: A Step-By-Step Guide for Public Speaking*, copyright © 1987 by Carol J. Kent. Published in Nashville, Tennessee, by Thomas Nelson, Inc.)

Unless otherwise identified, all Scripture quotations in this publication are taken from the *New King James Version* (NKJV), copyright © 1979, 1980, 1982, 1990, Thomas Nelson Inc., Publishers. Other versions used include: the *New American Standard Bible* (NASB), © The Lockman Foundation 1960, 1962, 1963, 1968, 1971, 1972, 1973, 1975, 1977; the *HOLY BIBLE: NEW INTERNATIONAL VERSION* (NIV®), Copyright © 1973, 1978, 1984 by International Bible Society, used by permission of Zondervan Publishing House, all rights reserved; *THE MESSAGE* (MSG). Copyright © 1993, 1994, 1995, 1996, 2000, 2001, 2002, 2005. Used by permission of NavPress Publishing Group; the *Holy Bible, New Living Translation* (NLT), copyright © 1996. Used by permission of Tyndale House Publishers, Inc., Wheaton, IL 60189. All rights reserved; and the *King James Version* (KJV).

Kent, Carol, 1947 —
    Speak up with confidence : a step-by-step guide for speakers and leaders / Carol Kent.
        p.   cm.
    Originally published : Speak up with confidence! : a step-by-step guide to successful public speaking. Nashville : T. Nelson, c1987.
    Includes bibliographical references.
    ISBN 0-89109-991-3 (pbk.)
    1. Public speaking--Religious aspects--Christianity. I. Title.
    [PN4121.K346 1996]
    808.5'1--dc21   96-47523
                                                   CIP

Printed in the United States of America
2 3 4 5 6 7 8 / 13 12 11 10

This book is lovingly dedicated to my parents,
Clyde and Pauline Afman.

You prayed for me since I was in the womb.

You led me to Jesus at an early age
and taught me to value the Word of God
as my authority and guidebook.

You taught me, by example, that serving Jesus
is more important than houses, land,
financial independence, or the acclaim of men.

You encouraged me to become educated and hard working,
but always dependent upon Him for power in ministry.

You are the spiritual backbone of all I am doing today
because you pray for me without ceasing.

You are loved.

Contents

Acknowledgments

With deep appreciation and heartfelt gratitude I acknowledge:

My husband, Gene: You are a servant to the emergence of my God-given gifts. Thank you for being my encourager, proofreader, and best friend.

My son, Jason Paul (J.P.): Your exuberant spirit and zest for life fill my heart with joy and meaning. This book has more humor because of you!

My sister Jennie Afman Dimkoff: You have supported me with love, prayer, and teamwork since the beginning of the Speak Up seminars. Thank you for proofreading the manuscript and offering valuable suggestions.

My friends Deborah K. Jones and Janet Fleck: You are women who know how to pray. You have taught me the absolute essential of bathing every project, every ministry opportunity, every phone call, and every page of this book in prayer.

My Speak Up staff: Your energy, expertise, and enthusiasm for sharing communication skills with others make the seminars possible. Because of you, ministry is being multiplied for the cause of Christ.

My prayer supporters Kay Jelinek, Maureen O'Neill, Susanne Rayner, Diana Pintar, and Marilyn Fenner: You have faithfully upheld this project in prayer, and I appreciate you.

My editor, Larry Weeden: Your valuable suggestions have made this project a better book.

PART ONE

Do I Have Potential for Speaking?

ONE

Speak? Not Me!

An Introduction

How many a man has dated a new era
in his life from the reading of a book.[1]

— Henry David Thoreau

After months of planning, we were on our way to the Grand Canyon! The first day was all that our family had hoped for. During day two, the temperature topped one hundred degrees, and the weatherman said there was no sign of a change in the near future. For two full days our seven-year-old son, J.P., had been saying, "Are we almost there yet?"

I was driving at the end of that second long day when we entered Amarillo, Texas. The sign on a local motel flashed Luxury for Less. Oh, I wanted that! The line underneath it was equally impressive: Clean and Comfortable. I wanted *that*, too!

My husband went in, put our money on the counter, signed the registration form, and obtained our room key. When we stepped through the door, we were mildly disappointed, but it *did* have beds and there *was* a shower — the two preestablished requirements for home away from home on this trip.

As we got the last suitcase out of the trunk and into the motel room, the top of the door fell off its hinge. Little Texas "critters" were making their way across the floor. The air conditioning had two levels, "very low" and "off"; but we were in cattle country, so an open window would have invited barnyard smells into the room. Turning back the covers on the beds, I discovered huge holes in the linens. (If you are from Texas, please don't be offended. I have visited your state on several occasions and realize you have many outstanding hotels. In this case, we had *chosen* low-budget accommodations.)

I wanted to leave, but my husband said, "We've paid our money, and we're staying!" It was one of those times when he had nonverbally said, "The end! Amen! Case closed! Don't bring it up again!"

By the next morning, the members of our happy, dynamic Christian family were barely speaking to one another. We silently packed the suitcases into the car, and with the exception of answering the questions of young J.P., we spent the entire last day of the trip with no laughter, no fun, no conversation, and no music.

Later that day we stopped at one of the viewing points along the south rim of the Grand Canyon. We parked the car and prepared to get our first glance of the sight. I was wearing sandals with heels on them, and I had every intention of putting on my tennis shoes, which were in the back seat.

At that moment my husband looked at me and broke the silence: "Surely you don't plan to see the Grand Canyon in high heels!"

Something in his tone made me decide that I *did* plan to see the Grand Canyon in high heels! We got out of the car and walked several feet toward the viewing point on very rocky terrain. I soon realized that I *could not* see the Grand Canyon in high heels.

I swallowed my pride and meekly asked my husband to retrieve my tennis shoes from the car. *Irritation* is not quite the word to describe what he was feeling at that point. *Exasperation* might come closer.

I'm sure Gene planned to throw the shoes *to* me rather than *at* me, but one of them hit me in the chest and the other one went flying beyond me. A young couple passing by us attempted to hide their amusement. In my humiliation I burst into tears, ran back to the car, and threw myself into the front seat as I shouted, "I've never wanted to see this dumb old canyon anyway. You and J.P. go look at it; I'll be waiting here in the car!"

My poor husband! We had traveled for three days in one-hundred-degree heat, and his wife was refusing to see the object of the entire trip. For several minutes he and J.P. stood outside the car waiting for me to quiet down and come to my senses.

Soon I heard our son say, "Daddy, *please* tell Mommy you're sorry!"

Since I wasn't climbing out, they decided to climb in. We had not begun the day with the Lord — it's very hard to have family devotions when the family members aren't speaking to one another. They said they were sorry; I said I was sorry; and together we told God how sorry we were for our terrible attitudes and lack of communication with Him and one another. As we finished, we exchanged hugs and shed a few more tears, this time for the right reason. I put on my tennis shoes, and hand in hand we started walking toward the canyon.

When we arrived at the edge of that gorgeous panorama of color, space, depth, and beauty, we were momentarily speechless. The pictures in *National Geographic* had not done it justice. I have never seen anything so breathtaking in my life!

We soon found out there was an echo in the canyon. Immediately, the words to a much-loved song of praise and testimony — "How Great Thou Art" — came to me. So we adapted the lyrics and formed a "yelling chorus." Holding hands and standing along the rim of the canyon, we shouted into that massive space, "O MIGHTY GOD, HOW GREAT THOU ART!" And we heard the creation echo back to the Creator the wonder and majesty of who He really is! It was one of the most spectacular moments of my lifetime, and I almost missed it because of a bad attitude.

WHERE DO YOU FIT?

Attitude is the key to success in public speaking as well as in vacations. Over the past few years I've had the privilege of training many people in the area of Christian public speaking. Each individual comes with a different attitude.

Some are totally optimistic. They've tried speaking and enjoyed it. People have commented on their concise, meaningful presentations or their excellent delivery. They have a positive attitude of anticipation that is accompanied by a desire to learn more skills for effective communication.

Others come with a hesitant attitude. These persons have often been thrust into speaking because of a role expectation or because no one else was readily available to do a job. With feelings of inadequacy, these individuals have reservedly agreed to speak. I have greatly enjoyed working with people who admit they need help. They always come with a teachable attitude and are quick to implement suggestions for improving content and delivery. And they *always* improve!

The "cod liver oil" attitude is demonstrated by persons who come to learn about speaking because of a paralyzing fear they desire to overcome or because relatives or friends forced them to get help. There is hope for these people. I have observed some extremely shy and withdrawn individuals become excellent communicators when they master the basics of public speaking and depend on God's power for energizing their message.

Only a handful of people have an arrogant attitude. Fortunately, I have never had to deal with them because they don't ask for help. They already know everything. Some years ago I read the following definition in a newspaper: "Oratory is the art of making deep sounds from the chest seem like they are important messages from the brain." Yes, there are a few individuals who speak with bombastic authority but have very little of lasting importance to say. For the Christian who desires to grow in the ability to communicate for God's glory, there is no room for this attitude.

Take a few minutes to read through the following comments. Are any of your attitudes reflected here? Check any responses that apply to you.

"Not Me!" Attitudes

- ☐ "I've never been good at speaking."
- ☐ "I don't have a college education, so I probably don't have anything worthwhile to say."
- ☐ "My voice sounds terrible on a recording, so why should I bore people by making them listen to me?"
- ☐ "If I can't be the best at speaking, I don't even want to try."

"Why Me?" Attitudes

- ☐ "I'm only teaching this class because no one else volunteered."
- ☐ "My husband's a pastor, and the people of this church expect me to lead the women's Bible study even if I don't feel qualified."
- ☐ "There was a time in my life when I was excited about teaching, but lately I've run out of ideas and function more out of obligation than joyful service."

"Yes, Lord!" Attitudes

- ☐ "I love God's Word and would like to be able to teach it more effectively."
- ☐ "I've been asked to give my testimony and would like to organize the events of my life in an understandable manner."
- ☐ "Even though I've been speaking for years, I know there is always room for more creativity in my presentations."
- ☐ "I'm a beginner and no one has even asked me to speak, but I want to get prepared to serve the Lord in the best possible way."

You may be as excited about learning how to speak as I was about seeing the Grand Canyon that summer. Or maybe you've never been asked to speak, but you've had an inner stirring (the Holy Spirit's nudging) that has stimulated you to prepare for doing God's work in the best possible way.

You may have tried speaking, experienced failure feelings, and determined to leave that job for someone else. Or you may already be doing some teaching or speaking, but you feel in need of more variety and creativity. Or you may be a seasoned speaker, eager for a few fresh ideas and new illustrations. No matter which description fits you, this book can help you.

Several years ago I got caught up in the spiritually debilitating exercise of comparing myself with other speakers. God had begun to open doors for me to speak as a workshop leader at several major conferences where I heard some of the finest Christian speakers in the country. I instinctively found myself comparing my content, style, and audience appeal with theirs. Then began the mental game of "If only . . ." It went like this:

- "If only I could tell humorous illustrations like he does, I would be an effective speaker."
- "If only I could teach the Bible like she does . . . maybe it's her British accent; if I could master that accent . . ."
- "If only I could tell deeply moving stories of real life experiences like she does . . . perhaps I should sit on a stool and generate intimacy with the audience. . . ."
- "If only I had a more authoritative voice like . . ."
- "If only I had a dramatic life experience . . ."

For a while I tried imitating the styles and methods of many of my favorite Christian communicators. The result was more laughable than effective. Every time I used the verbal and physical artistic expressions of someone else, I appeared artificial, and I concentrated more on *performing* than on *ministering*. Most of my spiritual growth spurts have come on the heels of such miserable failure. What a relief it was to realize that it was okay to be me!

I began developing the material for this book when it became apparent that there were people in my Bible study and in my church who had tremendous potential for speaking but didn't know where to begin. Not knowing *how* to organize a talk was a big problem for most of them, but the greatest hurdle of all was *fear*!

According to the *Book of Lists*, the number one fear of people in the United States today is public speaking. This paralyzing emotion has held too many people in bondage too long. I am convinced that the quality of every individual's life and ministry can be enhanced by learning a few basic principles on how to *speak up with confidence*!

John Wolfe, president of a communications training organization, says, "We won't remove your butterflies entirely; we'll just get them to fly in formation!" Whether you are a beginner or a pro, this book will teach you the secrets of becoming a more successful public speaker. You will learn

- How to find a topic and develop an outline
- How to use illustrations effectively
- How to deliver a talk with appropriate body language, vocal variety, posture, and gestures
- How to get started in Christian public speaking
- How to introduce someone
- How to preside over a meeting
- How to guide a discussion
- How to put your personal testimony together
- How to teach the Bible with clarity
- How to organize and file speaking materials

The purpose of this book is not to produce cookie-cutter communicators, all polished and perfect models of the manual. The purpose is to help you, within the framework of your own personality and God-given abilities, exalt the Lord Jesus Christ and communicate His truth in the most effective way. The person who knows the power of God and is willing to give his or her potential to Him will live in the humble realization that God often allows the person with little natural ability to do His greatest work.

TWO

Moses, Me, and Other Unlikely Public Speakers

Ordinary People with an Extraordinary God

*God does not require that each individual
shall have capacity for everything.*[1]

—RICHARD ROTHE

As I travel around the country, I'm sometimes amazed to see whom God has chosen to lead great organizations or to head up large retreats and conferences. Often, the individual isn't someone I would have picked. It overwhelms me to see that God is not at all limited in getting His work done because of an insufficient number of people with great personal charisma or dynamic speaking ability. He most often uses the willing servant who knows his or her weakness, and then when God blesses, there's no question about who gets the glory.

WHOM DO YOU IDENTIFY WITH?

Have you ever wondered if you are fit to guide that discussion group, to teach that class, to speak for a weekend retreat, or to lead a certain group of believers? What kind of people *does* God choose for leadership?

As you read through the following list of people God picked to be His representatives, put a check next to the name of the leader you most identify with. Underline the qualifications, fears, or emotional responses of these Bible leaders that are similar to your own. (Please start marking up this book. I never feel like a book is mine until I've highlighted, underlined, and circled ideas and have put my own comments in the margins.)

1. Moses
- The man chosen by God to lead the children of Israel
- A man without natural speech ability

When it comes to a reluctant public speaker, there is no finer example in Scripture than Moses. He had absolutely *no* desire to assume a position of leadership. Listen to his response when God called him to lead the Israelites.

> But Moses said to God, "Who am I that I should go to Pharaoh, and that I should bring the children of Israel out of Egypt?"
>
> So He said, "I will certainly be with you." (Exodus 3:11-12)

> Then Moses answered and said, "But suppose they will not believe me or listen to my voice; suppose they say, 'The LORD has not appeared to you.'" (4:1)

Have you sensed his lack of enthusiasm for public speaking?

> Moses said to the LORD, "O Lord, I have never been eloquent, neither in the past nor since you have spoken to your servant. I am slow of speech and tongue."
>
> The LORD said to him, "Who gave man his mouth? Who makes him deaf or mute? Who gives him sight or makes him blind? Is it not I, the LORD? Now go; I will help you speak and will teach you what to say." (Exodus 4:10-12, NIV)

If you identify with Moses, have you found a challenge in these verses yet? Many sad things are recorded in the book of Exodus, but one of the saddest is the comment that follows: "But Moses said, 'O Lord, please send someone else to do it'" (4:13, NIV).

Acts 7 records that Moses was a man mighty in words and deeds and that God used him in tremendous ways. But wouldn't it have been interesting to see how God worked through his weakness (public speaking) had he chosen to be instantly obedient instead of letting Aaron do the talking?

2. Miriam

- A type A personality from a godly family with a heritage of faith
- A prophetess who was a key leader in the great exodus of her people out of Egypt
- A leader who was jealous of the authority of Moses, her brother, and was publicly chastised by God

Miriam was a leader and a woman of influence during a time in history when few women held positions of authority. Micah 6:4 says, "I brought you up from the land of Egypt. . . . I sent before you Moses, Aaron, and Miriam." Not only was she a leader, but Scripture describes her as a prophetess and says that "all the women followed her." Wow! It sounds like she had it made. But the sad truth is that Miriam got fed up with the leadership of her little brother Moses (who was the leader of the people God had clearly appointed) and longed to usurp his authority. She even involved their brother Aaron in her cause.

Miriam's story is a sad one, because although she had been remarkably used by God in her lifetime, she took her eyes off her heavenly Father and concentrated on criticizing the leader God had chosen and promoting herself instead. God had to deal harshly with her in order to get her attention and to remind her He was the Lord.

Miriam's story is valuable for those of us in leadership positions.

How much better to learn from her mistake than to make it ourselves! The key is to remember that we are representing our Savior and not ourselves, and even when we are frustrated with a leader, to approach the matter in a way that honors God. Have you ever found yourself evaluating your boss and finding him or her lacking? Do you ever struggle to give those in authority over you the respect due them?[2]

3. Joseph
- A suffering saint
- A man with great ability who was put on hold for years

Genesis 37 through 50 records the life story of this extraordinary leader. He was the beloved son of his father, Jacob. Joseph was the recipient of the coat of many colors and had the ability to foretell the future through dreams. His brothers were envious, and one day when Joseph came to see them in Dothan, they cast him into that lovely Hilton-on-the-Plain, "The Pit." Along came Ishmaelite Tours, Inc., complete with live camels, and Joseph was sold into slavery. He wound up in Egypt in the home of Potiphar, the captain of the bodyguard, and became a trusted servant. Mrs. Potiphar falsely accused him of trying to take advantage of her, and Joseph was thrown into the palace prison for two years! Finally, through his ability to tell the future through dreams, he was elevated to prime minister of Egypt and was able to save his own family from famine during the years that followed.

Joseph suffered through the pressures of people, place, Potiphar's wife, prison, and position. If you have struggled through physical hardships, misunderstandings, temptations, leadership problems, or major moves in your life, take a long look at Joseph's reactions to the many change points in his life.

On the average, Americans move approximately once every five years. Have you ever moved to a home in a new area and no one recognized your talents? Did you ever know in your heart that you were capable of teaching or speaking, but you had no opportunity to use your gifts? I wonder what went through Joseph's mind during the two years he was in prison with no promise that his circumstances would change for the better.

4. Peter and John
- Unschooled, ordinary men
- Men who had been with Jesus

As a leader in Christian organizations and for a time as director of women's ministries in a large local church, I have interviewed numerous people for positions in Christian leadership. It never ceases to surprise me that people without Bible school or university training seem to think that they have no right to teach others or to accept up-front responsibilities. The overall response can be summed up with, "But I'm not really qualified to do what you're asking."

Remember what happened when Peter and John were jailed for healing a lame man and teaching the people and proclaiming in Jesus the resurrection of the dead? Acts 4 records that they had to appear before the Sanhedrin and answer hard questions the next day. Peter was empowered by the Holy Spirit and gave a powerful response stating that it was by the name of Jesus Christ of Nazareth (the One they crucified, but the One God raised from the dead) that the miracle was done.

Acts 4:13 is a classic verse for any of you readers who have given excuses for not proclaiming His truth because of your lack of education: "When they saw the courage of Peter and John and realized that they were unschooled, ordinary men, they were astonished and they took note that these men had been with Jesus" (NIV). When the Sanhedrin commanded them not to speak or teach at all in the name of Jesus, the men replied, "We cannot but speak the things which we have seen and heard" (4:20).

If Jesus could use these uneducated men to turn their corner of the world upside-down, surely He could use you. What's your response?

Does your heart burn with the good news to the point that you cannot help speaking about what you have seen and heard?

5. Paul
- Highly educated
- Christless background

In terms of education, Paul was the complete antithesis of Peter and John.

> If anyone else thinks he may have confidence in the flesh, I more so: circumcised the eighth day, of the stock of Israel, of the tribe of Benjamin, a Hebrew of the Hebrews; concerning the law, a Pharisee; concerning zeal, persecuting the church; concerning the righteousness which is in the law, blameless. (Philippians 3:4-6)

Talk about credentials, Paul had them! He was intelligent, energetic, and educated, but he had a Christless background. After his dramatic conversion on the road to Damascus, he knew where the real power for ministry comes from.

> When I first came to you, dear brothers and sisters, I didn't use lofty words and impressive wisdom to tell you God's secret plan. For I decided that while I was with you I would forget everything except Jesus Christ, the one who was crucified. I came to you in weakness—timid and trembling. And my message and my preaching were very plain. Rather than using clever and persuasive speeches, I relied only on the power of the Holy Spirit. I did this so you would trust not in human wisdom but in the power of God. (1 Corinthians 2:1-5, NLT)

The day I received my master's degree in communication arts from Western Michigan University was a milestone. I definitely had a sense of pride connected with seeing my name on the official diploma that I had earned by hard work and dedicated effort. A few years earlier I had earned my BS degree in speech education, but this was different — *this* piece of paper meant a higher paycheck and more prestige among my peers in the field of education.

In the middle of my moment of glory, my dear, praying mother had a long talk with me. She had been observing the many doors God was opening for me as a speaker. It was apparent that I would need to leave classroom teaching if I were to continue accepting the numerous invitations to speak for conferences and retreats. Mother looked at me, her firstborn, with love and deep compassion as she said, "Carol, God has given you a wonderful opportunity to obtain training as a speaker. You know how to make people laugh and how to make people cry." She paused, and then with poignant strength, she went on, "Don't you ever *dare* stand in front of an audience without being spiritually prepared and prayed up!" What important advice that is! Paul knew the secret. He said, "I consider everything a loss compared to the surpassing greatness of knowing Christ Jesus my Lord" (Philippians 3:8, NIV).

6. Joshua
- A leader who initially thought he might have a job that was too big for him
- A senior saint with a heavy assignment

Joshua was chosen by God to lead the children of Israel after the death of Moses. What a task! The last verse of Deuteronomy says it all: "For no one has ever shown the mighty power or performed the awesome deeds that Moses did in the sight of all Israel" (34:12, NIV). How would you like to follow someone like that?

There's something exciting about beginning a work for God — fresh enthusiasm, eager anticipation, new life, steady growth! It's another story when you are given the job of following a much-loved, effective leader and the congregation of the church or the participants in the Bible study measure you against their dearly departed favorite teacher of all time.

No wonder in Joshua 1 we read God's instruction to this newly appointed leader, "Be strong and courageous," *three* times in *four* verses. Listen to what God said: "Be strong and of good courage; do not be afraid, nor be dismayed, for the LORD your God is with you wherever you go" (verse 9).

I think Joshua's knees were knocking together. God didn't tell him not to be *nervous*; He told him not to be *terrified*. Have you ever said yes to an invitation to speak or to lead a group, and when the time came, you wondered if you had taken leave of your senses to have accepted such a responsibility? Look at what God did for Joshua: "The LORD exalted Joshua in the sight of all Israel; and they revered him all the days of his life, just as they had revered Moses" (Joshua 4:14, NIV).

Maybe you think you are over the hill when it comes to serving the Lord. Someone recently gave me this definition of the word *retired*: "I was tired yesterday, and I'm tired again today." Another friend shared this piece of trivia: "Life begins at forty, but it only lasts about fifteen minutes." My favorite goes like this: "You know your husband's getting older when a pretty girl walks by and his pacemaker makes the garage door opener work."

Whatever your *ancient* excuses might be, take heed. "When Joshua was old and well advanced in years, the LORD said to him, 'You are very old, and there are still very large areas of land to be taken over'" (Joshua 13:1, NIV). Don't you love it? God takes ordinary people (regardless of age) who are willing to do as He commands and uses them in extraordinary ways. I've had terrified people take the Speak Up seminar. I've also had people in their seventies go through the training. One participant started her first home Bible study after age seventy. Then she put her personal testimony together and shared her story at several Christian women's luncheons. God can use you, too!

7. David

- The least likely candidate for leadership
- A man mightily used in leadership after returning to God

"The LORD does not see as man sees; for man looks at the outward appearance, but the LORD looks at the heart" (1 Samuel 16:7). For years I heard that verse and even quoted it, but I never thought much about where it was placed in Scripture. Let's take a look at *why* it's in 1 Samuel. King Saul violated the Lord's instructions, and the Lord rejected him as king over Israel. Samuel was instructed to go to the home of Jesse and anoint one of his sons as king.

Visualize the events that followed. Samuel arrived in Bethlehem with a horn filled with anointing oil and a mission from God. He invited Jesse and his sons to a sacrifice, and then he reviewed the potential candidates for king. First came Eliab. After Samuel saw him, he said, "Surely the LORD's anointed is before Him" (1 Samuel 16:6). But God instructed Samuel not to consider the young man's appearance or height: "The LORD does not see as man sees."

Samuel continued to screen Jesse's sons for the Lord; six more passed before him. Finally, he asked Jesse if he had any more sons, and David was brought in from tending the sheep. God's choice was this youngest son, the one so unlikely to be picked (by human standards) that his father did not include him in the lineup. But he was God's man for the job.

God sees potential that you and I don't see on the surface. He often takes the person who has proved consistency in the "sheep-tending" jobs and moves that person into greater responsibility. What a great bit of advice that has been to me when I've had the job of interviewing discussion group leaders for Bible studies or selecting leaders in other places. While praying for wisdom, I'm not looking at the rising stars who at first glance look so well put together. I'm looking at who's been faithful at keeping the books, serving in the kitchen, or consistently encouraging others. I don't know who said it first, but it's still true: The servant of God is not the one reaching for the *top*, but the one reaching for the *towel*.

We cannot leave this discussion of David without remembering the dark moment in his days of leadership. Second Samuel 11:1 sounds like the opening line of a historical novel: "In the spring, at the time when kings go off to war . . ." (NIV). The true account of what happened that spring involved intrigue, romance, an extramarital affair, a pregnancy, a deception, a murder, a broken heart, and the death of a newborn son. Sin always has dire consequences.

You may wonder if God could ever use a person with a past like yours. Read Psalm 51. It's David's response to God after the prophet Nathan came to him following his sin. Listen to his plea:

> Generous in love—God, give grace! Huge in mercy—wipe out my bad record. Scrub away my guilt, soak out my sins in your laundry. I know how bad I've been; my sins are staring me down. (verses 1-3, MSG)

Can you feel the depth of his guilt?

> God, make a fresh start in me, shape a Genesis week from the chaos of my life. . . . Bring me back from gray exile, put a fresh wind in my sails! . . . I learned God-worship when my pride was shattered. Heart-shattered lives ready for love don't for a moment escape God's notice. (verses 10,12,17, MSG)

Following David's confession, he was a *forgiven* man. God used him mightily in leadership and gave him a second son by his wife Bathsheba. The boy's name was Solomon, and he became the third king of Israel.

If you've been living with "invisible ink" guilt for something in your past that you've confessed to God, accept His full forgiveness and get on with your life. Don't try to force yourself into leadership where you haven't been asked. Pray much, saturate yourself with the Word of God, and in His time, the right door for service will open.

8. Jonah
- A disobedient leader
- A man who got a second chance

When I was in junior high school, our family went through a major change. After church one Sunday morning, I noticed my father had tears in his eyes. That didn't occur very often, and I knew something serious was happening.

Dad put his arms around Mother and said, "I'm going to have to get out of church work completely or comply with God's will and go into the ministry where I belong."

In that moment Mother burst into tears, and the reality of what his words meant hit me! I was going to become a preacher's kid. That sounded like a death sentence to me. I knew that when I was a baby Dad felt God was calling him into the ministry. He went to Bible school for a while, but because of financial pressures he dropped out, intending to go back.

Years later, in fact, *five* children later, we had a new minister at our church. He began preaching a series of sermons on a man named Jonah, a man running away from God, physically and spiritually. My dad was miserable. In symbolic fashion he, too, was caught up in the belly of the whale, and he knew something had to change.

I watched as Dad enrolled in Bible school and then prayerfully went to see his boss, a man who did not know the Lord. Dad knew that all the agents in his insurance company were full-time employees, but that didn't stop him from making a special request. He asked his boss if he could continue working at part-time pay while he was going to school. The man leaned back in his chair and said, "I sure don't understand what this is all about, but as far as I'm concerned, you can continue here at your full salary while you're going to school. We'll watch what happens to your sales."

During the entire time Dad was finishing his education, he worked full time, and his sales were higher than they had ever been. Many were the appointments where Dad sold eternal life insurance along with the regular policies. Every need of our family was met, perhaps not with the abundance we would have liked, but every *real* need was met.

Those were exciting days. When I was fourteen years old, Dad took his first pastorate in a little railroad town in Michigan. There were forty-two people in the congregation, and seven of them were in our family. Everybody had a job. Since I had taken four years of piano lessons, I became the church pianist. I doubt that what I produced would have been called music, but it was a joyful noise. I could "plunk-thud" on "Dwelling in Beulah Land" a little better than the other songs in the hymnbook, so we sang that song every Sunday for weeks while I slowly added to my repertoire.

My father enjoyed visiting people in the local hospital. One day Dad met a man named Francis Kent, and he sensed that Mr. Kent was eager to know more about the things of God. A few weeks later, after Mr. Kent had gone home from the hospital and the Christmas holiday had passed, Dad asked me if I would babysit while he and Mother called on the Kents.

It was New Year's Day, my holiday from school, and I was not excited about babysitting. Mother had experienced a bit of a surprise when she was almost forty-two—and it wasn't menopause! You guessed it! The sixth child was born that year, the *fifth* daughter. The child born five years earlier was our only brother—a red-haired, freckle-faced boy, he was born on Halloween, with a disposition to match. Babysitting for this bunch was no small task. I grudgingly said I would take care of the children, and Mother and Dad went off to make their call.

They sat around the Kent's kitchen table with an open Bible and shared with Mr. and Mrs. Kent that God loved them, but sin separated them from Him. After my parents had clearly explained the gospel story, Mr. and Mrs. Kent were eager to invite Christ into their lives.

Before they prayed, Gene Kent, their seventeen-year-old son, stuck his head into the kitchen. He said, "I've been sitting in the living room and listening in on this conversation. Can I become a Christian, too?" The three of them got on their knees around that little kitchen table, with my parents at their sides, and invited Jesus Christ to be their Savior and Lord.

When Mom and Dad got home and told me that young Gene Kent had just become a Christian, I was too thrilled for words! My father was a strict disciplinarian. For years he had announced that there would be absolutely no dating of non-Christians for his five daughters. If you are from a small town, you can feel deep empathy for what that statement meant. At that point there were eight girls in the church youth group and two fellows. One of those young men was so unattractive you prayed he wouldn't ask you out, and the other one was so gorgeous you could get killed in the rush to get to him. Gene Kent—handsome, athletic, intelligent—was now a third possibility!

I love to tell this story, because that day while I was home doing the mundane, ordinary, not-very-much-loved job of babysitting, my mother and father were out winning my future husband to the Lord Jesus Christ. From that day to this, I often find that God does His extraordinary things in my life on my ordinary days. Sometimes life is so daily—but if we are spending time in the Word of God and in prayer, and if we are alert to the needs of other people, those ordinary days are filled with unexpected opportunity and fulfillment.

I'm so glad God put Jonah's story in the Bible. God used this man's spiritual journey to get my father back on track. Little did I know as a young junior high student that through the obedience of my mother and dad in following God's leading to a small church in a little railroad town, my own future husband would be won to Jesus Christ!

Maybe you are one of those people who has been given an opportunity to serve the Lord on numerous occasions and you've always run in the opposite direction. Now, in midlife, you're wondering if it's too late to respond in a positive way. It's never too late. God took Jonah and used him to turn Nineveh around. God took my mother and dad, with six children, uncertain finances, less education than they would have liked, and a zeal for God, and used them to evangelize a whole community—not the least of which was the man who became my husband. Give God the years you have left!

9. Esther

- A woman who was not raised in the home of her biological parents
- A woman who used her gift of influence to produce nationwide change

Queen Esther was a woman of beauty and wisdom whom God raised up "for such a time as this" (Esther 4:14). She was brought up by her father's cousin, Mordecai, after her parents' death. When King Ahasuerus wanted a new queen and Esther was selected as a candidate, she went through one year of beauty treatments to make a good first impression. After she was crowned queen, God used her to save her own people.

Throughout the book of Esther there is a beautiful picture of the underlying providence of God in preserving His people, the Jews, in the midst of a flood of anti-Semitism. The hatred of the Jews at this time was not so much a racial issue; it had more to do with their worship of God and their refusal to compromise on that issue (see Esther 3). The story of Esther is an outstanding illustration of God's working through the circumstances of our lives to do His purpose on the earth.

Occasionally, I have met people who make excuses for their lack of spiritual success by pointing to the negatives of their childhood homes or present circumstances. A woman came up to me one Sunday after a church service where my sister and I had sung a duet and shared in testimony. She said, "Carol, every time you and Jennie sing I have to fight a feeling of being angry with God. You came from a wonderful Christian home where you were loved and taught to serve the Lord from earliest days. My mother was an alcoholic, and my father was no good. I was never told I was loved, and I realize that's probably why I turned out to be such a failure."

Perhaps you, too, have been tempted to look at your difficult life situation or background, and you have decided to use a *legitimate* excuse as your reason for not growing spiritually or accepting Christian leadership. A few years ago a study was done on the backgrounds of the most selfless, powerful leaders in the world, and one of the common denominators was that they never blamed others for lack of success in their lives.

As Christians, we can make a difference. You may come from a home where there was physical and mental abuse, but because of Christ, you can be a positive example to your family today. Have you ever considered what would have happened if Esther had let her negative circumstances get her down? Her parents were dead, and she was a Jewish woman at a time in history when Jews weren't very popular. Had I been in her shoes (sandals?), I might have thrown a "pity party" instead of getting wise counsel and using all of my resources to produce positive change. Instead, at great personal risk, she used her gift of influence to protect her people from impending disaster.

Some of you may be called of God to become "issues" speakers. Whenever you read the paper or watch the news, your heart burns over the wickedness in the world, and you feel compelled to inform and motivate people to stand up for what's right and *do something*. Wow! Get to work! God may be raising you up, just as He raised up Esther "for such a time as this." You, too, can use your sphere of influence to hinder corruption and produce change.

10. Peter
- A man who frequently acted and spoke before he thought
- A man who learned self-control from the Master Teacher

Peter—what a delightful person to know! He always seemed to be in the middle of everything, and he kept the conversation moving right along.

Every group needs a Peter to bring out warmth and spontaneity.

In John 6:35 there is an account of Jesus teaching that He is the Bread of Life. Some of the things Jesus said were difficult for people to understand, and Scripture records that many of His disciples turned back and no longer followed Him.

This reminds me of a story I heard about an elementary teacher who assigned book reports on an animal story. One young student turned in a book report that was only one line long. He wrote, "This book tells more about penguins than I care to know." Some of the disciples in Jesus' day enjoyed watching His miracles and eating the bread He provided (see John 6:26), but when His teaching became difficult to understand, they left.

At that time Jesus turned to the Twelve and said, "You do not want to leave too, do you?" (John 6:67, NIV).

It was Peter who immediately responded, "Lord, to whom shall we go? You have the words of eternal life. . . . We have come to believe and know that You are the Christ, the Son of the living God" (John 6:68-69). How Peter's quick response must have warmed the heart of Christ!

Remember when Peter tried walking on the water, but he took his eyes off Jesus and began to sink? (See Matthew 14:28-32.) That same man, at the Mount of Transfiguration, enthusiastically wanted to build three shelters—one for Jesus, one for Moses, and one for Elijah (see Matthew 17:1-13). I enjoy being with people like Peter. Sometimes their follow-through is lacking, but they are so much fun and they have such dynamic ideas!

Matthew 26:69-75 records Peter's denial of the Lord Jesus. After the rooster crowed and Peter remembered Jesus' words to him, Scripture says, "He went out and wept bitterly" (verse 75). Earlier, Peter had said he would die rather than deny Christ (see Matthew 26:31-35).

Have you ever said anything you were sorry for? If you have struggled as a "motor mouth," you, too, have probably had moments of great joy and other times when you would have given anything to take back what came out of your mouth. Lila Trotman once said, "Lord, let me never enter a life except to build." If you read 1 and 2 Peter, you'll notice that Peter was a changed man. I can't help smiling as I read, "Be self-controlled" (1 Peter 1:13, NIV). He learned the lesson.

My parents gave me a Bible on my seventeenth birthday. I have long been an underliner and a note taker, and the margins of that old *Scofield Reference Edition* are filled with quotations and sermon outlines that touched my life deeply during late high school and then through the university years. One of those quotes is from F. B. Meyer: "You must be brought to an end of yourself before God can begin with you. But when once you have come to that point, there is no limit to what may be wrought during a single lifetime by the passage through it of His eternal power and God-head."

As we conclude these thoughts on Peter, don't focus on the big mistake of his life (or yours). Remember, when you've come to the end of yourself, God can begin His greatest work through you.

11. Matthew
- A meticulous person with great organizational ability
- A man who gave his potential to the Lord

Matthew was wonderfully organized. As you read through his gospel, you'll notice that he beautifully recorded the Sermon on the Mount in chapters 5 through 7. Then he listed the miracles, neatly packaging them together in chapters 8 and 9. The whole gospel of Matthew gives a thorough, systematic overview of the life and times of the Lord Jesus Christ. I can almost imagine Matthew in the group of disciples with a legal pad and a pen (or whatever they used in those days) in hand. He would have documented everything that took place. What a great addition he was to the Twelve!

A couple of years ago when I was teaching the gospel of Matthew, I saw it! *There*, right in the middle of the miracles, was the account of Jesus calling Matthew to be a disciple. There was Matthew, a tax collector, probably a man who skimmed a little of the profits off the top—if he was like other tax collectors of his day. He was certainly not a candidate for Christian Leader of the Year. But Jesus, walking by the tax office, looked at Matthew and knew he had all the potential of becoming one of the biographers of His life. Jesus said, "Follow Me," and Matthew got up and followed (see Matthew 9:9).

As God looks at you today, He doesn't just see what you *are*—He sees your *potential*! Second Peter 1:4 says, "For by these He has granted to us His precious and magnificent promises, so that by them you might become partakers of the divine nature, having escaped the corruption that is in the world by lust" (NASB).

Bob Benson, in *Come Share the Being*, notes that being a "partaker" of God's divine nature means that we can "share in the very being of God." Benson says:

Do you remember when they had old fashioned Sunday school picnics? It was before air-conditioning. They said, "We'll meet at Sycamore Lodge in Shelby Park at 4:30 Saturday. You bring your supper and we'll furnish the tea." But you came home at the last minute and when you got ready to pack your lunch, all you could find in the refrigerator was one dried up piece of baloney and just enough mustard in the bottom of the jar so that you got it all over your knuckles trying to get to it. And there were just two stale pieces of bread. So you made your baloney sandwich and wrapped it in some brown bag and went to the picnic. And when it came time to eat you sat at the end of a table and spread out your sandwich. But the folks next to you—the lady was a good cook and she had worked all day and she had fried chicken, and baked beans, and potato salad, and homemade rolls, and sliced tomatoes, and pickles, and olives, and celery, and topped it off with two big homemade chocolate pies. And they spread it all out beside you and there you were with your baloney sandwich. But they said to you,

"Why don't we put it all together?" "No, I couldn't do that, I just couldn't even think of it," you murmured embarrassedly. "Oh, come on, there's plenty of chicken and plenty of pie, and plenty of everything—and we just love baloney sandwiches. Let's just put it all together." And so you did and there you sat—eating like a king when you came like a pauper.[3]

As I think about how *little* I bring and how *much* He brings and how He invites me "to share in the very being of God," I could weep. It must be what F. B. Meyer meant when he said, "There is no limit to what may be wrought during a single lifetime by the passage through it of His eternal power and God-head." I want that. My whole being longs to make a difference; yet, as Benson says, there are some of us running through life, hanging on to the stale baloney sandwich, and saying, "God's not going to get what I have! No sirree!" It isn't so much that He can't get along without your baloney—you need His chicken!

SELF-EVALUATION

1. Which of the Bible characters discussed in this chapter did you most identify with? If you are studying this material as a group, have each person tell how he or she identifies with one of the Bible leaders.
2. What are your greatest strengths as a speaker and/or leader?
3. What do you perceive to be your greatest weaknesses?
4. Spend some time in prayer. Are you willing to dedicate yourself, your known abilities, and your potential to the Lord? Ask Him to give you an attitude of anticipation as you get better prepared to serve Him.

PART TWO

How Do I Prepare a Talk?

THREE

If You Don't Know Where You're Going, You'll Probably Wind Up Somewhere Else

An Overview of How to Prepare a Talk

Aim at nothing and you'll hit it—every time!
—ANCIENT INDIAN PROVERB

One of the most worn-out books in my office is the atlas. With its missing cover, dog-eared corners, and coffee stains, that atlas has elicited comments such as, "Carol, don't you think you could afford a new one this year?" or "Your atlas does nothing to affirm your image as a professional speaker" or "The pages of these maps are so marked up and worn out I don't know how you can figure out where to go."

Actually, I received a brand-new atlas recently, and I did *try* to use it. After a few trips, I reverted to the old one. The experience was like renewing an acquaintance with a comfortable old friend—reliable, familiar, trustworthy, dependable, and much more.

The atlas performs two major functions for me. First, the opening page gives me an overview of the continental United States. When someone calls and asks me to speak out of state, I can look at the big map and have a general understanding of where I'm headed and how far away I'll be. Second, when the commitment is made and the day of the engagement draws near, the pages for the specific state enable me to follow exact instructions to reach the appointed location. Of course, I could print

MapQuest directions, but I still like the feel of my trusted atlas.

In much the same way my atlas helps me with directions on a trip, the main points of my outline for a speech give me the overview of where I'm headed. The subpoints "fill in the blanks" with additional information and illustrations that will make the specific direction and application of my talk clear and meaningful.

Look at the chart on the next page, "Building a Speech," and then we'll discuss how to begin putting a talk together. (At the end of chapter 6, I've included a complete example of one of my talks and how it was put together.) There are several major things for you to consider before you actually write the outline for your speech.

DISCOVER AN IDEA

Every speech starts with an idea. You've picked up this book because you've had ideas worth repeating, and you'd like to be able to communicate them with skill and confidence. Your idea for the speech you're going to outline may not be well developed or have much structure to it yet, but you'd like to pursue working on it.

DRAW ON GENERAL KNOWLEDGE

Most beginning speakers make an amazing observation. When brainstorming about what they have to speak about, they discover that there is so much material to draw from, the real problem is not to think up potential topics and illustrations, but to eliminate all but the best. Read through the following list, and think about specific incidents, sayings, or people that flash into your consciousness. Train your mind to use these vast resources for speaking material:

- Nationality (What do you know about your grandparents?)
- Childhood (Where did you live? What were your hobbies? Who are your siblings?)

THE OVERVIEW

Building a Speech

ATTENTION-GETTING RAPPORT

Attention Step

I. _____
   A. _____
   B. _____
II. _____
   A. _____
   B. _____
III. _____
   A. _____
   B. _____

APPROPRIATE ILLUSTRATIONS

I. _____
   A. Definition
   B. Anecdote
II. _____
   A. Personal Experience
   B. Quotation
III. _____
   A. True Story
   B. Biblical Example

BALANCED OUTLINE

I. _____
II. _____
III. _____

NARROW TOPIC

Consider:
• Audience
• Aim

GENERAL KNOWLEDGE

• Nationality
• Childhood
• Parents
• Children
• Education
• Job Experience
• Church
• Bible Study
• Books
• Observation

IDEA

APPLICATIONS

CONCLUSION

REMEMBER   PRAY • PLAN • PRODUCE • PERUSE • PRUNE • PROJECT

- Parents (What values did they instill in you?)
- Children (How many do you have? What have they taught you?)
- Education (Who was your most memorable teacher? Why?)
- Job experience (What skills have you mastered? Who were your employers?)
- Marital status (Have you ever been in love? Have you experienced rejection or loneliness?)
- Church (What Christian leaders influenced your life in a profound way? How is life different because of teachings you were exposed to?)
- Bible study (What parts of the Bible are you the most familiar with?)
- Books (Which books have helped you shape your values and attitudes? How?)
- Observation of people (What qualities do you desire in a friend? What have you learned about life and Christianity from other people?)

The next chapter will teach you how to take a variety of personal experiences and formulate meaningful illustrations and applications that could be used in a personal testimony, message, or speech. You have more to say than you might think.

DECIDE ON A TOPIC

Once you realize that you *do* have potential for speaking and that you have a lifetime of memories to help you with illustrations and general background for your talks, your most important decision will be to choose a specific topic. Make this decision a matter of prayer, and then ask yourself the following questions:

1. What do I know a lot about? Make a list of your hobbies, specialized training you have received, or certain topics that you've done extensive reading on. Author Phillip Keller took his background as a shepherd and did an in-depth study of Psalm 23. He painted a word picture of our role as the sheep and God's role as the Master Shepherd, and the Christian community experienced Psalm 23 in a new way. *A Shepherd Looks at Psalm 23* has become a classic on that portion of Scripture. It is extremely important for speakers as well as writers to choose a topic they know a lot about.

You may be feeling sorry for yourself because you aren't a leading authority on anything. Take heart! Experts say that if you will read on one topic for one hour a day for five days a week for five years, you will become an expert in that field. There's hope for you if you are willing to get started.

Commit yourself to becoming a student of the Scriptures. The Bible is your best reference book. Every part of your ministry will be enhanced by a deeper knowledge of God's Word and an understanding of how to apply scriptural truth.

2. Do I have an urgency to speak about it? Do I feel enthusiastic about sharing my ideas with someone else? Occasionally, I have sat in a Bible study or attended a Christian gathering where the speaker strolled to the lectern with bowed shoulders (conveying lack of confidence and zero enthusiasm) and said something like this: "Well, I really haven't had much time to prepare this week, but if you will all turn in your Bibles to John 15, somehow, with God's help, we'll all get something out of this." Immediately, the audience is psychologically prepared for boredom. There is an instant awareness that even the speaker is not interested enough in the subject to prepare to speak on it. The commentary is particularly tragic when the unenthusiastic leader is handling the Word of God. When you choose a topic, select something that you are eager to work on and that people have a desire to know more about.

3. Does anyone want to hear it? You may be an expert on something that most people have no desire to know more about. You might have training in a specialized technological field, or perhaps you know every bit of baseball trivia since the beginning of the game. A few groups of people will listen to you, but for the most part, the general public will not come out with record attendance to hear you address those topics.

To get a very good idea of what topics interest people, glance over the magazine covers as you stand in line at the grocery store or pharmacy. Thousands of dollars have been spent on research to determine the topics the general public will spend money to read about. This is very helpful information for the Christian speaker who desires to prepare material on topics that will interest people in knowing biblical solutions to today's problems. Some popular topics include:

- Life after death (The Bible has a lot to say about this one!)
- Diet, exercise, and nutrition (There is always an audience for this topic.)
- Secrets of success (Read the book of Proverbs. You'll be an expert on God's view of success in no time.)
- Dealing with stress (If you have experienced much stress, you are an expert in this field. There is nothing so powerful as a personal illustration of experiencing God's answer to stress.)
- Meaningful relationships (This is a topic that touches every human being, and the Bible is full of practical advice on how to cope.)
- Time management (Who doesn't need encouragement in the area of organizing our days and giving our life's energy to something that ultimately counts?)
- Pet care (Don't laugh! This topic has been in the *top five* of what people want to read about. Obviously, we would not put together a Christian talk entitled "Is There a Doggie Heaven?" but knowing that people like to read about animals does tell me that illustrations about pets will be well received.)

The psalmist said, "My heart is stirred by a noble theme . . . my tongue is the pen of a skillful writer" (Psalm 45:1, NIV). Begin a list of your topic possibilities; review the list often and keep adding to it. The following questions will help you determine good subjects to develop:

- What do you read about in your spare time?
- What subjects do you research on the Internet?
- What are your hobbies?
- What were your favorite subjects in school?
- What current events do you feel strongly about?
- What gets your attention — in the newspaper, on the radio, on television, and on-line?
- What and who inspires you?
- What entertains you?
- What part of God's Word do you know well enough to teach others?
- What topic motivates you to read, research, rant, rejoice, record, redo, and on and on? What do you have a *zeal* to talk about? What makes you weep and pound the table? Do you feel strongly enough about anything to spend hours preparing to speak about it?

Look at the topic wheel on the next page that includes a number of possible topics. Put a check mark next to each topic that you know enough about to develop into a talk. This wheel is only a small sample of the hundreds of possible topics.

As you do this exercise, think about other topics you could address. For now, list five topics you could begin to work on. Some may be from the wheel; others will be a product of your own brainstorming. Make prayer a major part of the process when choosing your topics. You will spend many hours on a well-prepared message, and the content needs to be something you feel compelled to speak about.

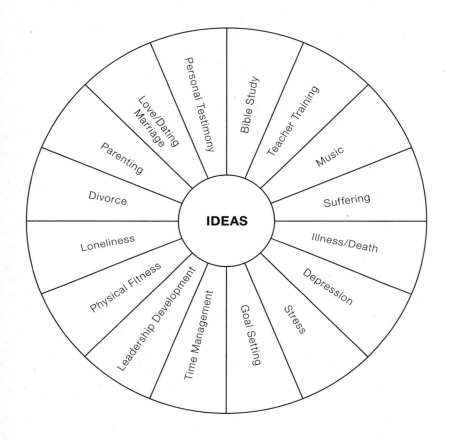

Topics I could develop:

1.

2.

3.

4.

5.

Before we leave this discussion, it's important to note that occasionally you, as a Christian speaker, will need to address unpopular topics. It's never *fun* to speak on the sin problem, but it's necessary to teach "the whole counsel of God" (Acts 20:27), and dealing with "worthless idols" (sin—Jonah 2:8) is part of that. Two significant biblical examples of this would be Jeremiah and Jonah.

How would you like to be told by God that you have been selected as His main public speaker and your job will primarily involve uprooting, tearing down, destroying, and overthrowing as well as building and planting? That's the situation Jeremiah faced (see Jeremiah 1:4-10). I know myself well enough to know that I'd love the building and planting part, but the negative message I'd rather leave to somebody else!

Jonah is the first foreign missionary mentioned in Scripture, and we discussed his disobedience and his second chance in chapter 2. When he began running in step with God, Jonah was given a very short text for his evangelistic campaign in Nineveh: "Forty more days and Nineveh will be overturned" (Jonah 3:4, NIV).

As a speaker-trainer and as a very optimistic person, I usually encourage speakers to prepare a message of hope. Had I been the speechwriter for Jonah, I would have suggested a more delicate opening line. Here's where we see the importance of relying on God's direction as topics are chosen and as messages come together. God knows *who* is in the audience and what it will take to get the attention of those people.

As we read on in the third chapter of Jonah, we are instantly aware that God's message through Jonah got results. "The people of Nineveh believed God's message, and from the greatest to the least, they declared a fast and put on burlap to show their sorrow" (Jonah 3:5, NLT).

DESCRIBE YOUR AUDIENCE

The topic you develop first will be determined by your audience analysis. Will you be talking to Christians or non-Christians? The most important single factor in deciding *what* to speak about is knowing *who* is going to be in the audience. The following questions will help you decide what kind of presentation would be most appropriate:

Who?

- Can you describe the age, sex, background, and nationality of the group?
- Are there resource people, magazines, or books that could help you better understand the audience?

What?

- What denomination or organization unites these people?
- What topics have been addressed at their past events?
- What speakers have they had recently?
- What are their hopes, struggles, fears, needs, and questions?
- What are their common interests?

Why?

- Why did they ask *me* to speak?
- Am I an expert on the subject they want to know more about?
- Why are they here? Are they a "captive audience" (university chapel), or are they here by choice?

How?

- How will I get their attention?
- Are there recent statistics related to their needs that will help me prepare?
- What does the Bible say about the answers to the questions they are asking?
- Is this group geared to visual learning (data projector, videos, and/or handouts), lecture/discussion, or straight lecture?
- How much time do I have?

After answering these questions, you are ready to pick one of your topics and get to work.

DETERMINE YOUR AIM

The next important factor in putting together any talk is determining your aim. What do you want to cause your audience to *do* as a result of hearing your message? Sometimes people talk in circles because they really haven't identified their aim. The audience will never figure out the purpose of your talk if you cannot state your aim in one clear, concise sentence.

Tim Timmons, master communicator, shared this illustration in an article in *Leadership*:

> A fellow attended a special evening service at the church but sat near the door. After the speaker had droned on for some forty minutes, the fellow got up and left. On the way out, he met a friend coming in. The man asked, "Am I very late, Zeke? What's he talking about?"
>
> "Don't know. He ain't said yet!"

Timmons went on to say, "In every speaking situation what matters most is this: Did the audience get the speaker's point?"[1] It's important for the listener to be tactfully confronted with a choice: What will change in my behavior or attitude this week as a result of hearing this message?

Before developing an outline for your topic, write out an aim for your talk. Think about who your audience will be, and finish this sentence: "I want to cause my audience to . . ."

This aim is too vague: "I want to cause my audience to be more spiritual." There's no way to evaluate if the desired objective is reached. An aim needs to be measurable and doable.

Here is an example of a good aim: "I want to cause my audience to spend at least ten minutes per day reading the Bible for the next week." This aim is specific and has a time factor built in. It will be difficult for the listener to avoid the bottom-line questions: Am I in the Word daily for even a short time? Will I commit myself, for at least a week, to reading the Bible every day? The audience could not remain neutral at the end of this message. Because the speaker's aim is very specific, the listener is faced with a definite choice. It is both measurable and doable. If your aim doesn't answer the question, ". . . by doing *what*?" it's too vague.

Speak Up speech coach Bonnie Emmorey says, "Another way to evaluate your aim is to look at the key verb. The stronger the verb, the more measurable the aim." Here is a list of verbs that can be measured.

Answer	Practice	Invite	Ask	Tell
Compare	Produce	Design	Share	Call
Memorize	Choose	Give	Help	Pray
Read	Accept	Encourage	Visit	Confess
Repeat	Describe	Explain	Express	Locate
Review	Schedule	Prepare	Develop	Share
Set up	Write	Support	Plan	Name
Define	Record	List	Create	Find

This list is not meant to be exhaustive, but it will give you a starting point. Today's busy audiences are less interested in being entertained and more interested in what they will gain as a result of listening to you. They want to know: How will this presentation help me in my everyday life?

If you are a teacher or speaker, look at the notes from your most recent presentation. Could you state your aim in one sentence? Remember, if you don't know where you're going, you'll probably wind up somewhere else!

François de Sales said it well when he remarked, "My test of the worth of a preacher is when his congregations go away saying, not, 'What a beautiful sermon!' but, 'I will do something!'"[2]

A good aim gives the listener "take-home" value by challenging the audience to follow through with a specific action step. Taking the time to develop a good aim will move your talk from being inspirational to becoming *transformational*.

DEVELOP AN OUTLINE

After a weekend conference a few years ago, I came home totally motivated and emotionally stimulated by a dynamic Christian speaker.
When my husband asked about the speaker's content, I said, "Well, he
was so funny, and he's such a superb storyteller."

"But what did he *say*?" Gene insisted.

Other than retelling a couple of humorous anecdotes, I couldn't
come up with any meaningful content. It's true—sometimes we need
a good, relaxing laugh. There are some outstanding Christian humor-
ists, and we know that laughter is physically good for us. However, if
your aim is to send people home after your presentation with worthwhile principles to live by, the message needs key points that are easy to
remember. That's one reason why outlines are important.

The very mention of the word *outline* sends shivers up the spines of
many people because the thought of having to organize material into
some form intimidates them. Don't make a tool into a task. An outline
is just a "systematic listing of the most important points of a subject,"
according to *Webster's New World Dictionary.* An outline doesn't have
to be complex to be effective.

Perhaps you feel comfortable with one style of outline and never
attempt anything new. Your teaching style is so predictable the audience almost knows what you are going to say and how you'll present
your material. In attitude we are sometimes like the sign posted on a
country road in the early spring: "Choose your rut carefully—you'll
be in it for the next thirty miles!" I've known people who have been in
a rut for thirty years, not just thirty miles. Why not get out of the rut
and try something new?

If you are a beginning speaker, you will soon make the exciting
discovery that outlining a talk is much easier than you thought. Having
even a simple structure for your content makes putting together a talk
much less difficult. A speech outline should be short enough that you
can remember it. If you can't recall your points, your audience will not

retain the main ideas in your message. Using bullet points instead of Roman numerals will make your outline more user-friendly to a post-modern audience. As you look at the following examples, ask God to give you one new idea that will help you bring creativity and clarity to your messages.

Using the Alphabet

Examples:

THE ABC's OF SPIRITUAL WARFARE
- The **A**rmor
- The **B**attle
- The **C**hampion

THE ABC's OF CHRISTIAN DATING
- Be **A**ccountable
- Be **B**iblical
- Be **C**ommitted

Acrostic — Take a key word from your topic and develop an outline around that word.

Example:

MAKE A DAILY DATE WITH GOD
D — Decide to do it
A — Apply the principles
T — Take the time
E — Enter His presence

Cause/Effect — This outline occurs naturally all through Scripture.

IF YOU DO THIS . . . THIS WILL HAPPEN.
Example: 1 John 1:9

If we confess our sins, he is faithful and just and will forgive us our sins and purify us from all unrighteousness.

The Repeated Word

Example:

3 STEPS TO A POSITIVE PERSPECTIVE
- **Step** Back (Reevaluate the situation)
- **Step** Out (Ask God to reveal His perspective)
- **Step** Up (Choose to be positive)

Repeated Word and Alliterative

Examples:

LIFE MAPPING
- **Travel** Plans
- **Travel** Partner
- **Travel** Particulars

CHOICES
- **Choose** to Listen
- **Choose** to Learn
- **Choose** to Live

Theme Style

Examples:

HE'S MY *ROCK* (WHAT HE HAS DONE)
I'M READY TO *ROLL* (WHAT I WILL DO)

ROAD TRIP! (USING SIGNS)

1. Stop
2. Do Not Enter
3. Wrong Way
4. Dead End!
5. Road Closed
6. Detour
7. Yield

If you end with Yield, it leads directly into your AIM. For example, I want to cause my audience to yield to biblical guidelines for dating.

For a shorter talk, cut down on the number of signs.

1. Stop
2. Wrong Way
3. Yield

Play on Words

Examples:

SON PROTECTION FACTOR (SPF)

- Stand Firmly
- Prepare Carefully
- Fight Victoriously

THE FORMULA FOR PEACE

No Christ = No Peace

Know Christ = Know Peace

Comparison Play on Words

Example:

Man's Way	→	Hopeless End
God's Way	→	Endless Hope

Rhyming

Example:

MAKE TIME FOR GOD!
- Create the Space
- Clean Up the Place
- Seek God's Face

Questions

Questions—this technique is easy and quick. In this chapter I organized the information on audience analysis with this method.

Example:

- Who is the author?
- To whom is he speaking?
- Why is he giving this advice?
- What is the application for me today?

Answers

Example:

What is forgiveness?
Webster's Dictionary: To excuse a fault or give a pardon

1. Forgiveness is a choice.
2. Forgiveness has a cost.
3. Forgiveness cancels a debt.

Verbs

Sometimes a passage of Scripture will easily provide a "natural" outline via key verbs.

Example: Ephesians 5:1-21 (NIV)

- BE imitators of God (verse 1).
- LIVE a life of love (verse 2).
- BE pure (verses 3-7).
- LIVE as children of light (verses 8-14).
- MAKE the most of every opportunity (verses 15-16).
- BE filled with the Spirit (verses 17-20).
- SUBMIT to one another (verse 21).

How to

Almost any workshop topic could be developed with this style of outline. I would use numbers instead of Roman numerals for this one.

Example: How to Raise Christian Kids

1. Sharpen your own personal convictions.
2. Devise a set of biblical parental objectives.
3. Realize relationships always precede rules.
4. Spend time with your children.
5. Keep your promises.
6. Train children in survival skills (manners, grammar, and stewardship.)
7. Live your convictions consistently.

Comparison

List opposites or the negatives and positives of your topic.

Example: Message based on 1 Corinthians 13:

- Love is . . .
- Love is not . . .

Character

Use any Bible character and profile that person's life.

Example: Joseph's Pressure Points, using alliteration

- People
- Place
- Passion
- Prison
- Position

Numbers

Using numbers in the title and outline gives the audience an immediate idea of where you are headed and how long you will be speaking.

Example: Four Attitudes That Will Change Your Life

1. Humble Attitude
2. Contrite Attitude
3. Merciful Attitude
4. Teachable Attitude

Your Outlining Challenge

- Get Ready
- Get Set
- Grow![3]

Have fun experimenting with different outlines. Practice putting together words that help you think in outline form. A friend and staff member of the Speak Up seminars wrote, "Thank you for your *care*, *concern*, and *consistency*." What a great outline! It's a word outline (all nouns), and it's alliterative (all points begin with C).

I left this note for my son when he was ten years old:

WHO?   J.P. (Jason Paul)
WHAT?   Please clean your room.
WHEN?   Before dinner
HOW?   With great energy and enthusiasm
WHY?   Because you love your mother and want your allowance.

I Love You!
Mother

Outlining can even make parenting fun!

The mailman delivered a letter from a special friend. She said,

As I think about you writing a book, I am convinced that God will use that process to teach you many things about yourself and His power within you. In addition to all He plans to do in your life, there is His plan to touch the lives of so many more people as they read the final product. It's exciting for me to pray about the potential impact this book will have. Let me know if there is ever anything I can do to help via *prayer*, *proofing*, or *prodding*.

By this time you are so skilled at thinking in outline form that I don't even need to point out the great outline in this letter.

1. ***Be brief.*** Keep your outlines *short* for most inspirational talks. People will be more likely to remember your points if they are not lengthy. The only exception would be when you are teaching an inductive Bible study class where people are coming with their notebooks open, ready to take careful notes and do more intense study.

2. ***Be simple.*** Use words that people understand. Keep your points couched in everyday terminology. Don't try to show off your outstanding vocabulary or your theological superiority

by making your outline too technical.

3. *Be visual.* If it's possible to use PowerPoint or to print your outline for the participants, do so. People *love* outlines and automatically think you are organized and well prepared if an outline of your talk appears on a screen or is handed to them.

4. *Be correct.* If you use PowerPoint, be sure words are spelled correctly.

Let me illustrate the fourth guideline. I was finishing preparations for a lecture on a day when I was short on time. My PowerPoint presentation was hastily prepared, but completed in the nick of time. Secretly, I was feeling a little smug for having accomplished so much. After my presentation, the floor was open for questions. In front of three hundred people, the first person I called on said, "Carol, did you know you misspelled a word on the third point of your outline?"

Color me *red* (with embarrassment)! My topic was "Speak Up with Confidence!" and the woman shot a huge hole in my self-esteem. I was there to train *them* how to do a professional job of speaking confidently for the Lord, and I came off looking like a poorly prepared presenter. It was my own fault, and I've learned to proofread my handouts and PowerPoint presentations before making them public property!

This may seem picky, but as your opportunities for speaking grow, there will always be a grammarian in the audience who "tunes out" if your outline is faulty. Correct form is easy to master and makes you look more professional.

5. *Be willing to grow.* If you have always used a sentence outline, try an acrostic or an alliterative outline for your next talk. If you speak to the same group on a weekly basis, they will love the variety, and you will be praised as the most creative teacher they have ever had! It's well worth the extra effort—not just for them, but for your own growth.

The next three chapters will help you fill in the subpoints on your outline. Are you having fun yet? Your work has just begun, but this could be the start of the biggest growth spurt of your Christian life. Chapter 4 will help you develop personal illustrations. A message without illustrations is like a Christmas tree without lights. The purpose of telling illustrations is to give heart and soul to an otherwise sturdy but colorless outline. You are about to learn the secret of the best speakers in the country—demonstrate with illustrations.

FOUR

Big Lips and Other Beauty Marks

The Art of Developing Personal Illustrations

The best speaker is he who turns ears into eyes.[1]

—OLD ARAB PROVERB

It happened in the fourth grade. I was sitting in my seat looking intently at my teacher, priding myself—as always—on being a good student. John, in the seat behind me, tapped me on the shoulder. I'd been noticing him for quite some time, hoping he would notice me, too. I turned around in my seat, put on my best smile, and said softly, "Yes?"

He didn't say anything; he just stared at something on my face. Then he elbowed the fellow next to him and whispered, "See?"

This fellow also began to stare at something on my face and replied, "Yeah, I see."

The initiator of the conversation then proceeded to say, "She does have big lips, doesn't she?"

I was devastated! I turned around in my seat, pretending it didn't matter, all the while breaking out in a nervous red rash. Finally, the bell rang, and I ran outside, boarded the bus, and found a quiet seat in the back.

When the bus stopped in front of my house, I jumped off and ran in the front door and up the stairs to my second-story bedroom; I threw myself across the bed and sobbed. I knew I was the homeliest girl in the entire world. I was certain I'd never be asked out on a date. I knew

I would never be married. In our culture, no dates mean no proposals. And I also doubted that I would ever be gainfully employed. Who would hire a girl with lips like *these* to work in a business establishment?

When the initial hurt subsided, I decided that to be one of the achievers in life, I'd have to become one of the thin-lipped people. Whenever I had leisure time, I would stand in front of my vanity mirror and painstakingly roll my lips inward until they were thin and beautiful. But I discovered a brand-new problem: It is almost impossible to speak with "thin" lips (at least with big lips rolled in to look thinner)! I began practicing at home with my "new" mouth, trying to perfect my speech before making a public debut.

One day my father looked at me and said, "Carol, what on earth are you doing to your mouth?"

I said, "What do you mean, Dad?" In my effort to look pretty I hadn't even noticed how distorted my speech was with this new, "attractive" mouth.

As you've been reading this story, perhaps you've been thinking about your own fatal flaw. For you, it might not have been big lips, but perhaps you had a nickname that labeled you in a negative way. Perhaps your voice cracked in the middle of a solo, and you have never sung publicly again. Perhaps you tripped on your way up to a microphone, and the humiliation of that moment has kept you from accepting a leadership position again. All of us have areas of vulnerability and personal failure that allow an audience to see how "real" we are and to identify in some way with what we have gone through.

DEFINING THE PURPOSE

Illustrations make truth memorable. They help people "see" the point we are trying to make. Illustrations move people from the outline to the heart of the talk. Long after the message has been given, people will recall the applications and main aim of the talk because of a captivating key illustration.

Years ago Walt Disney discovered an important ingredient in successful feature-length animated cartoons. *Snow White* was a huge success, but other films that followed, although equally well constructed from a technical viewpoint, never did as well. Disney's team tried to analyze what made the difference. They made an incredible discovery! Every one of the truly successful productions, the films that people would pay to see again and again, had two ingredients — laughter *and* tears! Everything they did from that point had to have both elements before it was released.

That discovery is important for a speaker. Every time I put together a talk and prayerfully insert the illustrations, I check for a balance between laughter and tears. My aim is not to send people home sobbing nor to have them laughing so hard that they miss the seriousness of the message. But I have discovered that people listen more closely and make more life-changing decisions when my illustrations include a variety of warm humor and meaningful experiences. It's a winning combination!

GETTING STARTED

Before you think about the outline or structure of a talk, it's good to give your brain a stimulating assignment — just to get your "gears" in motion. All of us have come to this point in our lives with a well-stocked filing cabinet. Into this cabinet over the years have come all kinds of valuable material from which illustrations can be drawn. It includes information we have read, responses to people and events, happy times, sad times, family traditions, vacations, job experiences, and so on. Where is this cabinet located? Right on top of our shoulders. I continue to be amazed as the Speak Up seminar is presented, and people begin to discover the wealth of information for speaking that they already have at their disposal.

You have a considerable amount of material that simply needs to be remembered and developed. I hope you are getting excited, because by the end of this chapter, you could have enough ideas to capture the attention of audiences for a lifetime.

Paul said, "And I want you to know, my dear brothers and sisters, that everything that has happened to me here has helped to spread the Good News" (Philippians 1:12, NLT). Almost everything that has happened to you has the potential of helping other people grow spiritually. If you've had more failure than success, as a speaker you may have even more to draw from, since most audiences are made up of fellow strugglers who will identify with a person "in process" rather than one who has already "arrived."

Step 1. Start by dividing your life into chapters. Take individual sheets of paper, and write any of the following headings that apply to you. If you keep a notebook or journal, keep these pages there so that you will be able to add thoughts regularly.

- Stage 1: ages 1–5 — What do you remember of your early childhood? (nicknames, things your parents or other relatives said about you)
- Stage 2: ages 6–12 — What do you recall about elementary school? (teachers, classmates, nicknames, toys, collections, hobbies)
- Stage 3: ages 13–18 — Describe your memories of junior high and high school. (first date, awkwardness, self-concept, first job, spiritual growth)
- Stage 4: ages 19–22 — What did it feel like to enter the adult world? (the college years or your first full-time job, marriage, decision making about the rest of your life)
- Stage 5: ages 23–30 — How did you adjust to marriage or singleness? (conflicts in relationships, childbirth, financial problems, fatigue, time pressure)
- Stage 6: ages 31–40 — Do you like who you grew up to be? (family trips, marker-moments, traditions, holidays, children in sports, music lessons, conflicts during children's teen years)

- Stage 7: ages 41–50 — What are your midlife questions and answers? (describe grandparenting, high school and university reunions, evaluation of life's choices)
- Stage 8: ages 51–65 — Have you experienced any crisis points with health or relatives? (transitions in relationships, hobbies, and ministry opportunities)
- Stage 9: ages 65 and over — How are you adjusting to retirement? (new opportunities for travel and volunteer work, fears regarding health or financial security)

Step 2. Write down a word, phrase, or sentence that reminds you of significant events from these time periods. You don't have to see a spiritual application at this point or analyze why that event is memorable. Simply brainstorm about the "pictures" your mind has collected over the years. You have so many of these mental images tucked away that you will have sufficient illustrative material for years of speaking once you unlock the memory bank and get to work on the next few steps.

Step 3. Choose one personal experience that might make a good illustration in a message or talk. Answer these questions about the illustration you select:

- What emotions did I experience while living through this chapter of my life?
- What spiritual lesson did I learn from this experience?
- What Scripture verse or passage comes to my mind as I meditate on what happened?
- How could my willingness to tell this story help another person?

Step 4. Write out your personal experience. It should include the following elements: a line to get the audience's attention; a concise description of what happened; a verse or a scriptural principle that helped; and an application for the audience (a statement or a question).

MAKING USE OF YOUR PAST

Now let's really get to work. Following are several "trigger" words or phrases that could fit into one or more of the seasons of your life. Think about these words and the people, events, or experiences they bring to your mind. Insert any possible illustrations on the appropriate sheet in your notebook or journal. I have presented these ideas in two sections. The first gives you questions and comments to help you think of something from your life that could be developed into an illustration. The second is an example to show you how to identify an incident from your past that could be developed.

NATIONALITY

What are your roots? Is your nationality known for being unique in some way? (Romantic? Hard working? Plain and proper? Strong in faith? Good cooks? Loud and obnoxious? Musical? Pioneering?) Do you identify with some part of your heritage? Have you blamed your bad habits on your nationality? What slogans did you grow up with that have their "roots" in your nationality? Are there tasteful anecdotes you could use?

I am 100 percent Hollander. On my mother's side, my grand-father came over from the Netherlands and settled in the Grand Rapids, Michigan, area. My father's family is of Dutch descent as well. One of my grandfathers was the *dominie* (or minister) of the Netherlands Reformed Church, and Mother had many stories to tell us of life in the parsonage, enduring the Dutch services (three on every Sunday), dating a Christian young man who was not Dutch Reformed, falling in love, and then facing her father in the parlor after eloping. We always heard, "If you're not Dutch, you're not much!" Our hardwood floors were so clean that open-heart surgery could have been performed on their hand-waxed surface.

When I'm speaking in a part of the country where there are lots of Dutch people, it's always a good rapport-builder to refer to my background. People immediately relax and say to themselves, *She's one of us!* and they are ready to listen. Know your audience well enough to be aware of when you can use your background to help gain their attention. Also, be alert enough to know when mentioning your background could hinder your rapport.

Keep in mind that many ethnic jokes would never be appropriate to use in any public presentation. Even if your intent was purely for humor, someone in the audience might misunderstand and miss the whole point of the message because your comment was interpreted as a slur. If I have a question about whether or not to use a joke of this nature, I ask a trusted Christian leader for advice. Usually, if I have to ask, I already know the answer. Why risk something that might not be appropriate when there is so much excellent material that *can* be used?

BIRTH

Where were you born? What were the events surrounding your birth? What was the financial status of your parents at the time?

I was born sidetracked. My mother and father did not have medical insurance when they were expecting me, and the doctor instructed them to wait until after midnight to come into the hospital if Mother went into labor in the evening hours. That way they would avoid having to pay the charges for an extra day; patients paid for a *full* day even if they were there only a few minutes of that day.

Predictably, Mother went into labor after the dinner hour one evening. Her labor pains grew in intensity, and by 11:00 p.m. she was not at all sure that the baby was going to wait until after midnight. My father is a good man and a wonderful support person, but never one to spend a dime needlessly. Mother packed her bags, and Dad s-l-o-w-l-y drove her to the hospital. When they arrived, they sat out front while Mother had additional labor pains and Dad watched the clock.

Finally, at five minutes to midnight, they walked up the steps, stopped for Mother's contractions along the way, and registered as the clock struck twelve. One hour and ten minutes later I was born. No wonder I have problems getting sidetracked. I was almost born on the steps of the hospital!

As you think of your own illustrations, alert your mind to possible transitional statements or applications. For this story, I might say, "In my Christian life, when I feel disorganized and things are not getting accomplished in the right time frame, I'm often tempted to shrug my shoulders and say, 'That's just the way I am. Why, I was born sidetracked. It's been the story of my life!' Have you ever been caught blaming circumstances and events of the past for your present failures? There's hope for people like you and me."

CHILDHOOD

What nicknames were you called as a child? Where did you place in the birth order? Did you feel loved? Were you abused or neglected?

My "big lips" illustration is a classic example of this category. Every time I share that story I get an immediate response. Sometimes I will be greeted after the message with, "Oh, honey; your lips don't look so bad." Or "Did you know that people with full lips stay looking younger longer?" Actually, today I like my lips, and as maturity eases the pain of childhood hurts, most of us find the application for life that fits this kind of illustration. This illustration identifies a "universal need" or "common bond" between people that hits all age categories. Every human being has experienced low self-esteem in some area of life, and by sharing this story, I am able to make truth memorable for a lot of people. Today I get mail lovingly addressed to "Big Lips Kent," and there are many letters in my files from people who experienced similar situations or comments and reacted in various ways. Look for the "felt need" in every personal experience — the key ingredient that will allow people to see themselves in your illustration.

SUMMER CAMP

Do you remember giving your counselor the most exciting challenge of the summer? Did you make a life-changing commitment at camp? Did you ever work as a camp counselor?

I spent part of my summers between university years counseling at a camp for girls in crisis. One summer I had the daughter of a migrant worker in my cabin. Her name was Maria. She spoke very little English and stayed close beside me.

One sunny day our camp director suggested that we take our campers to the Happy Mohawk Canoe Livery. When we arrived, I told the camp director that since I had never been canoeing before, it might be wise for me to be in the last canoe so I could observe the others.

Shy Maria looked at me and said, "I can't swim. Can I be in your safe canoe?" I told her to hop in, and we started paddling down the river.

We managed our canoe just fine until we reached a fork in the middle of the river, and I saw that the canoes in my party were going down the right-hand side of the fork. I had no idea how to steer a canoe.

While Maria and I struggled to follow the others, we crashed into the embankment in the center of the river. The branches of a tree were arched over our canoe, and I looked up to see a long, slithery snake on a branch just above our heads. I'm a veteran camp counselor and have endured frogs in sleeping bags, spiders on cabin walls, mosquitoes, and fire ants, but snakes immobilize me! But as I saw the desperate look in Maria's eyes, my maternal instinct must have risen to its highest level. I leaned over, grabbed one of the paddles, stood up, and swung! To this day I have no idea whether or not I actually hit the snake. In that split second the canoe went over, and within a few more seconds it was caught in the current and going downstream fast, followed by our life preservers and paddles.

Maria was several feet away from me, splashing her arms and yelling, "Help me! Help me! I can't swim!" She went under water.

I was kicking my feet, flailing my arms, desperately trying to get to my camper, but getting nowhere fast in the strong current. Maria's head came up a second time as she screamed, "Please help me! I'm drowning!"

Panic was setting in. Her head went under. I looked to the right, saw two men coming in a canoe, and began to yell with full vocal force: "Help us! We're drowning! We're drowning!"

Time goes slowly when you're drowning. It seemed to take thirty minutes for the men to get to us, but it was probably more like thirty seconds. They finally arrived and paused for a brief moment to watch me continue to splash frantically. One man calmly asked, "Hey, lady, why don't you just stand up?"

When I quit struggling and stood up, I found out I was in three feet of water. When Maria came up for what appeared to be her last breath on this earth and saw me standing, she stood up and was saved, too!

I swallowed my pride and said, "Thank you very much." I had almost drowned in three feet of water because I didn't have sure footing.

DEVELOPING SPIRITUAL APPLICATIONS

Here's where some of us have a problem. We have many great events as a part of our past, but we haven't worked out the spiritual applications. Let's walk through the instructions given in Step 3, using the canoe story as an example.

- What emotions did I experience while living through this chapter of my life? (fear, panic)
- What spiritual lesson did I learn from this experience? To find spiritual "sure footing" by faith in the Lord Jesus Christ instead of trying to save myself.
- What Scripture verse or passage comes to my mind as I meditate on what happened? "God saved you by his grace when you believed. And you can't take credit for this; it is a gift from God. Salvation is not a reward for the good things we have done, so none of us can boast about it" (Ephesians 2:8-9, NLT).
- How could my willingness to tell this story help another person? In other words, what is the transitional statement and application that will enable people to apply this illustration to their lives?

I have worked with women in conferences and retreats for a number of years. I was also employed as director of women's ministry at a large church in Fort Wayne, Indiana, prior to moving to Michigan, and eventually to Florida. One by one I have had women walk through the doors of my office or come to me for counsel and say, "Carol, there's something missing in my life. My husband gets on my nerves, but I think he's normal. I'm learning to forgive my kids for being thirteen and fifteen years old. To tell you the truth, I don't think the problem is them; it's me! There's a void in my life that nothing seems to fill."

These women are a lot like I was on the day of the canoe mishap. They've been struggling to save themselves by being the best possible wife, caring mother, and baker of casseroles for the neighbors; some have even been involved in church activities, trying to fill the vacuum on the inside by working hard to merit God's favor. What they really need is to realize the truth of Ephesians 2:8-9. It's not by works and good deeds that we become Christians and earn heaven; it's by grace—simple faith in the Lord Jesus Christ, His shed blood on Calvary for our sin, and His resurrection—that we can experience new life. Have you been struggling to save yourself, or have you experienced the truth of God's Word and the reality of saving faith? Do you have *sure footing* in Him?

At the conclusion of each illustration think of a key question or statement that will penetrate the hearts of the listeners. Remember, as a Christian speaker, you want them to catch the heartbeat of the illustration and choose to respond by personalizing the application and making a positive change in attitude or behavior.

BRAINSTORMING FOR MORE PERSONAL ILLUSTRATIONS

You are beginning to get the idea of how to construct meaningful illustrations from a lifetime of personal experiences. As you read through the following words and phrases, write notes about any possible illustrations you could develop for future talks in the space following each suggestion.

1. Music Lessons

Most of us took music lessons at one time or another. What did you learn about discipline as a result of this experience? Did anything unusual happen at one of your recitals? Have any of your children struggled through piano lessons? Build illustrations on your musical successes and/or failures.

2. Education/Teachers

Where did you go to school? Who were the teachers that had a profound impact on your life, both positively and negatively? One person told me that for eight years in a country school she had a teacher who didn't like her and never made her feel special. The experience greatly affected her life and has become a major illustration for speaking.

3. Athletics

What sports did you play? Were you outstanding in a certain athletic event or sport? What are the rules of the game, and are there spiritual parallels that you could draw? Were you unathletic, and did you always feel inadequate in sports? Did you experience being the last one picked when your teammates chose up sides for softball and football? Many excellent Scriptures link spiritual experience to an athletic event, and the applications are numerous.

4. Dating/Marriage

Almost everybody loves a love story. Think back to your dating and courtship days. Did you have any painful experiences that have later proved to be humorous? My husband proposed to me in a cemetery; he gave me my diamond engagement ring above a rushing river while we sat on railroad tracks; and to this day he has made variety and creativity watchwords in our marriage. Our first apartment was in a building that had at one time been a funeral parlor. Few stories hold interest for the female listener as well as a true story of romance.

5. Job Experience/Leadership Roles

During my high school years, I worked in a small retail store for a man who had been in charge of prisoners of war during World War II. He ran the place like an army sergeant! It wasn't a pleasant experience for me, but I did learn a great deal about how to respond to authority—a valuable spiritual lesson for the future.

My sister Bonnie Emmorey sometimes works for a supermarket chain as the "mystery shopper." She is hired by the owner to go into several stores with the specific purpose of trying to get away with anything she can. Her job involves trying to pass off outdated coupons as legitimate, sneaking merchandise out on the lower part of the cart without paying for it, and testing the attitudes of the employees by demanding specialized cuts of meat when they are busy with other things. In other words, the job involves checking the overall efficiency of the store's employees.

In the beginning Bonnie felt terrible about "stealing" things out of the stores, but each day it got easier and even started to be fun to see just how much she could get away with. Obviously, she was doing the job she was hired to do because the owner wanted to cut down on theft and better train his employees to function more efficiently. However, the lesson she learned has to do with the problem of sin in our lives. At first we experience guilt; then as we choose to continue in sin, it gets easier to fall deeper into the trap until we have almost no conscience about it. The application is obvious.

6. Children

Try keeping a journal of things your children or grandchildren say. If you're single, spend time around families with children. Your life will be richer, and you'll have a valuable source of illustrations.

I had been in California for a training seminar, and when I returned from the trip, our son, then five years old, came running to greet me. As I scooped him up in my arms and we whirled around in a big circle, he shouted, "Oh, Mommy, Mommy, when I saw you right now, it was just like I saw you brand-new!"

Wow! That was a moment when the application was immediate. As God looks at me through His Son's shed blood on Calvary, instead of seeing me in my sin, He sees me as *brand-new*—a forgiven woman.

7. Trauma/Illness

Some of the most meaningful spiritual lessons come out of the "valley" experiences of life. If you have gone through a difficult experience, ask God to help you focus your application on the hope that is ours because Jesus lives. Sometimes the details of a trauma tend to overshadow the more important point of what God allowed you to learn as a result of the experience.

8. Family

Brainstorm about family traditions, collections, hobbies, reunions, and events. What have you learned about relationships as a result of living in your family? There is a wealth of illustrative material in this category.

9. Vacations/Travel

When you go on trips, take notes about the interesting places you see and people you meet. When my husband and I visited the San Francisco Bay area, we toured Alcatraz Island and had the experience of being locked up in solitary confinement. It was for only one minute, but the experience was one of complete darkness and total silence. It felt like the longest minute of my life, and I have a new understanding of what the Bible means when it talks about darkness.

A few years ago, I toured the FBI headquarters in Washington, DC, and I took notes on everything. Later that week during my Bible study teaching lecture, I shared up-to-date information taken from the "Crime Clock" on how many violent crimes had been committed so far that year. It was a powerful example of the fact that we do have a sin problem.

10. Special Events

Another valuable source of illustrations comes from the uncommon days of your life. Our family just attended a birthday party for my husband's ninety-year-old grandmother. Grandma is hard of hearing and has difficulty seeing as well as she used to. She spends much of her time in a wheelchair, but her mind is as sharp as ever.

We arrived at the convalescent home where she resides and joined a room full of well-wishers. As our turn came to greet Grandma, we hugged and spoke our congratulations, followed by my husband's jovial question, "Grandma, have you had any problems with the men in this place chasing you down the hall?"

"As a matter of fact," Grandma replied, "the man who stays in the room next to mine got into bed with me last week."

In shock, I questioned, "Why, Grandma, what did you do?"

With a twinkle in her eyes, she quickly retorted, "I yelled, 'Help! Help! This man's in the right church, but he's got the wrong pew!'"

Grandma stole the show! After all, it was her party! When we started for home, I wrote the event in my journal and began brainstorming for applications. Have you ever needed help, and you didn't know where to turn? Have you ever felt out of control?

11. Christian Growth

List the highlights of your walk with the Lord. Who influenced your life in a meaningful way? What books, in addition to the Bible, have helped to mold you? Have you experienced any setbacks in your spiritual journey?

REMEMBERING GUIDELINES

This chapter has highlighted information on how to develop the most powerful illustrations you have to work with — key stories from your life. The audience always responds to speakers who have *experienced* the principles that they are talking about. Stories, anecdotes, and quotations from other sources are necessary to bring balance to a talk, but the audience always seems to remember personal illustrations longer than anything else.

Chapter 12 will give you information on where to look for other types of illustrations, and you will learn how to file the valuable resources you have collected. For now, remember these simple guidelines:

1. Be sure of your facts. In this day and age of mass media, your illustration could go around the world via the Internet or in a digital or video format. Once a woman asked me about the credibility of a well-known speaker. The facts of a key illustration in her presentation were different from the recorded version the woman had listened to the week before. What a reminder that was for me to be certain of my details and consistent with my repetition of a true story.

2. Don't present a fictional story as if it were true. In one of my favorite illustrations, I begin by saying, "I'm from a family of great storytellers. Have you ever had a story at your house that got better every time it was told?" From the beginning, the audience knows I'm about to tell an *exaggerated* version of an actual happening. By passing off a great story as your own experience when it is taken from a book or another speaker, you destroy your credibility in front of those who know better.

3. Be certain the story fits your aim. You will occasionally run across a story that "begs" to be told. Discipline yourself to make sure the illustration does not overshadow the point. Don't "bend" the application to fit a great story.

4. Get permission from family members or friends before telling an illustration about them. People have come up to my husband and son saying, "Wow! We sure know a lot about you!" If you are teaching a local Bible study, your teenager may not want stories about his or her life to be discussed on a public platform. Before I use illustrations about other people, I make a point of asking for their okay. There may be some excellent stories with superb applications that you can't use until a later date—like when your child is grown and is no longer self-conscious.

5. When possible, give credit to the originator of the story or cite the source. Many great stories have been passed around so long we don't know where they came from. In that case, get right into the story. If you are giving credit, make a brief comment about the source so that the beginning doesn't sound like an apology or a lengthy explanation. However, if you are citing a source of unquestioned authority, such as a scientific report, a recent research project, or a respected person's quote, people will "listen up" when you tell where the information came from. Learn to recognize when the citing of a particular source will add credibility to your talk.

6. Never use another speaker's story if you are speaking in his or her territory. A couple of years ago I was invited to speak for a large retreat. A speaker friend confessed to me that when she spoke there the year before, she used one of my favorite illustrations. She said, "I knew you wouldn't mind. You probably got it from somebody else, right?" The truth was that it was totally original and had taken a lot of time and work to develop. I felt "robbed" of one of my best stories, although imitation is still the sincerest form of flattery!

Before using another person's material, ask yourself, *Is it likely that this speaker will ever address this group?* If the answer is affirmative, be kind enough not to use key illustrations you learned from that speaker. Even if you gave credit for the source, it would be inappropriate to use another speaker's best material if that person might be speaking to that same group in the near future.

On one occasion I was asked to speak to a group, and the person who called said, "Carol, when you come, please don't give your message on attitudes. Last month I transcribed that message from one of your CDs and shared it with our women, so you'll want to give them something fresh."

7. Adjust the length of the illustration to fit the time you have to speak. If you have only fifteen minutes to speak, it would be inappropriate to spend ten minutes developing *one* story. What is your aim? If the illustration cannot be abbreviated to make your point in a shorter time, choose something else. Perhaps a quotation, proverb, definition, or description would work just as well as a story.

8. Write out your illustration word for word when developing a new story. This helps to get rid of redundancy. It gives you a chance to paint the best visual picture for the listener by choosing colorful nouns and verbs that make the story come to life. Never read from your manuscript when telling the story. The right words will flow, even without memorization, if you've done your homework ahead of time.

9. Carefully write out your transitional statement so it leads into the application of your story. Many motivational speakers tell humorous anecdotes that are primarily meant to entertain an audience. Because I am a Christian, my reason for speaking revolves around an important aim. Never ad-lib the statement following your illustration. What point are you making? Choose wording that helps the audience understand the meaning of the story.

10. Videotape new illustrations and critique yourself. Ask these questions: Did I use too many words? How could I tell this story better? Is my application clear? Does my body language enhance the story?

The first few times I use an illustration, I'm constantly reworking the wording until it *feels* right. The result is worth the effort! People will always identify best with your personal illustrations if you are vulnerable about your failures. They don't want to hear about how perfect you are. They want to know that you, like them, have made wrong choices or devastating mistakes, and with God's help, you got back on track. Be authentic.

DOING AN ASSIGNMENT

Develop one new illustration following the formula given in the first part of this chapter. If you are studying this book with a group, share the illustrations with one another the next time you meet. Ask for affirmative comments as well as suggestions for improvement. If you are reading on your own, record the illustration and critique yourself. Have fun, and don't be surprised if you actually *enjoy* speaking!

RECEIVING FEEDBACK

Occasionally, an illustration brings an unusual response. This quote came from a letter addressed to "Big Lips Kent":

> Dear Carol,
> . . . I thank God for your big lips because through them I heard for the first time that God loves me. The day you shared your testimony in Toronto, Ontario, I prayed with you and received Jesus Christ as my personal Savior. . . .
> Love,
> A Grateful Friend

Receiving a letter like that makes the work involved in preparation seem like a small investment compared to the return.

FIVE

Start with a Bang!

Gaining Rapport

*It is the same with men as with donkeys: whoever would hold
them fast must first get a very good grip on their ears.*[1]

— RUSSIAN PROVERB

I love chocolate! I've told my husband that when I die, I'd like to
be dipped in chocolate and then shipped off for burial in Hershey,
Pennsylvania. I live in a house with two other chocoholics, so I have to
have special hiding places for it. I keep some in the refrigerator; there's
almost always some in the freezer; I keep a little in the Halloween treat
candy jar on the top shelf of the cupboard; and a tin labeled Borwick's
Baking Powder usually contains semisweet chocolate chips.

Recently, I was at home on an ordinary day. I planned to spend
the entire day preparing for some major speaking engagements. After
jumping out of bed, I donned a pair of old slacks and a faded, well-
worn sweater. I hurriedly brushed my hair, and I didn't put on any
makeup. I hesitate to admit this, but even relatives might not have
recognized me that day. My sister Paula has a makeup case with print-
ing on the side that says, "My face is in this bag!" I needed that bag! Do
you have the picture?

Sitting down at my desk, I opened the Bible to Matthew 5, the
text for my next retreat message, and I began a careful reading of the
Beatitudes. I came to verse 6 and read, "Blessed are those who *hunger*."
What do you guess I thought about? Thinking quickly, I realized it

would be a small thing to go to one of my favorite hiding places and satisfy my overwhelming desire. I went to the refrigerator—no chocolate! I tried the freezer; it, too, was void of chocolate. There was none in the Halloween treat candy jar. I instinctively went to the pantry and pulled out the Borwick's Baking Powder can, knowing I had purchased chocolate chips just the week before. To my amazement, it was empty, and in the bottom of the can, I found a note in my husband's writing that said, "Sorry, honey, I beat you to it!"

I was disappointed, but thought quickly, *Obviously, the Lord doesn't want me to have any chocolate this morning.* I reluctantly went back to my desk to concentrate on message preparation. After fifteen minutes I thought, *Why, it's only three miles to the store. I could be there and back in no time at all and satisfy this ridiculous craving.*

After making the decision to go to the store, I caught a glimpse of myself in the mirror. If you've done much speaking in your hometown, you know you can't go anywhere without being recognized, and I didn't want to be seen in public looking like I did that morning. It took me at least half an hour to apply some makeup and put on appropriate clothing, so when I got to the store, I decided to make the trip worth my while. I picked up the largest Hershey's with almonds I could find; then I grabbed a giant-size Cadbury Caramello. (For those of you not into this sort of thing, that's chocolate and caramel together in one mouth-watering bite!) On my way to the checkout counter, I picked up the biggest bag of M&M's on the shelf.

As I walked out of the store and across the parking lot to my car, I consumed one-third of the Hershey's with almonds; on the three-mile trip home, I finished it off. I was fast moving into the Cadbury. Thinking quickly, I realized that the M&M's would taste terrific with a big pot of coffee. I envisioned a delightful study time, sipping coffee and eating M&M's, one by one, all day. As the coffee in my drip pot worked its way to the bottom, I continued devouring the Cadbury. When I heard the final gurgle, signaling that the coffee was ready, I was finishing off the last bite of the second sixteen-ounce candy bar. At that moment, I realized I was so sick, I could hardly move.

I'm ashamed to admit it, but that day, a day I had reserved for Bible study, prayer, and preparation for ministry, I wound up wasting hours of precious time over a ridiculous human craving. I don't know about you, but it's not always the big things that get me down. It's the little things, those self-defeating behaviors that leave me feeling out of control, like no kind of Christian leader at all, certainly not like an appropriate example to others of the "purposeful Christian life." Those are the moments when Satan whispers in my ear, "What right do you have to teach others how to live when your own human appetites are totally out of control?"

The entire verse goes like this, "You're blessed when you've worked up a good appetite for God. He's food and drink in the best meal you'll ever eat" (Matthew 5:6, MSG). Are you longing to go somewhere spiritually where you've never been before? Are you hungry for God's Word and for growth in your relationship with Him, or are you, like me, allowing human appetites to mentally, physically, and spiritually wipe you out? Today we're going to look at what the Bible says about God's prescription for a healthy appetite.

WHAT IS A RAPPORT STEP?

What you have just read is the opening illustration for a retreat message. Your first twenty-five words should be so well planned that you seize the attention of your audience. Within the first thirty seconds of your talk, the people in the audience have already decided if it's worth their time to listen to you.

Rapport is a French word (the *t* is silent) that means, in communications circles, "to gain the attention of your audience." It connotes the idea of agreement, harmony, or a sympathetic relationship between you and your listeners. The experts tell us that attention has three aspects: (1) an adjustment of the body and its sense organs (Could you *taste* the chocolate?); (2) clearness and vividness in consciousness (I hope you could immediately identify with me in that you, too, have experienced a situation where your appetite was out of control); and (3) a bent toward action (Since we have all had the problem, what does the Bible say about the solution?).

It's a fact that when you begin a talk by gaining the attention of your audience, you increase the listeners' capacity to hear what you have to say. If the beginning of your message is clear and vivid, the audience is ready to move toward action.

A good "attention step" should accomplish the following goals: capture attention; create warmth between you and your audience; surface needs of a group or an individual; and introduce the subject of your talk. You know your rapport is working when you feel the audience *anticipating* what you have to say next.

WHY IS RAPPORT IMPORTANT?

The phone rang. I picked up the receiver, and the woman on the other end of the line greeted me warmly and then said, "Carol, how do you get so many people to come to Bible study on time?"

I thought about her question and then replied, "I always begin with a *grabber*." Years earlier, as a participant in other classes, I noticed that teachers who waited for the stragglers started later and later. The class members soon realized that the *scheduled* starting time was not the *actual* starting time.

When I began teaching, I made a commitment to two essentials —starting at the appointed hour and beginning with a good rapport step. I opened each class with the most dynamic story, quotation, or creative visual I could think of that would tie in with my aim for that day. When people were late, others told them that they missed the best part of the lesson. People usually arrived on time after that.

As soon as you begin speaking, and sometimes even before you open your mouth, each person in the audience is thinking, *Why do I need to listen? What does this speaker have to say that will apply to me? Am I wasting my time? Will this be interesting?*

A writer for *Life* magazine, Paul O'Neil, said, "Always grab the reader by the throat in the first paragraph, sink your thumbs into his windpipe in the second and hold him against the wall until the tag line."[2] This advice is meant for writers and is a humorous exaggeration of the importance of immediately grabbing the attention of the reader, but there is also important truth here for the speaker.

The possibilities for effectively gaining the attention of your audience are as limitless as your own God-given creativity. I believe time in front of an audience is an awesome responsibility, and since God's work deserves excellence, I don't want to waste one minute.

The rapport step is one of the last things I prepare, even though it comes first in the talk. It's important that you have a thorough understanding of your content and overall aim first. Then you can plan an introduction that will be appropriate and will accomplish its purpose.

Always complete your rapport step with a carefully prepared *transitional statement* that will tie your opening into the subject of your talk. It's a very awkward moment for you as a speaker and for the audience as listeners if you've planned a spellbinding opening—and suddenly you pause, too long, trying to remember where you're headed and why you told the story.

Humor is probably the fastest and most effective way of gaining rapport with an audience. The Bible tells us, "A cheerful heart is good medicine" (Proverbs 17:22, NLT). An article in *USA Today* quoted Dr. William Fry, a Stanford University psychiatrist who has studied humor for thirty years. He points out some bodily benefits of laughter:

> Heart and blood circulation rates soar, imitating the effects of an aerobic workout. Afterward, these rates drop below average, promoting relaxation.
>
> Muscles vibrate, providing an internal massage that breaks up tension.
>
> The brain emits certain hormones that trigger the release of endorphins, the body's natural painkillers.[3]

In the book *The Joy of Working*, Denis Waitley and Reni L. Witt cite these findings:

> Recent discoveries in psychopharmacology relate directly to the theory of why a positive mental attitude is one of the single most important traits toward achieving health and happiness. Medical researchers have discovered that the body produces natural morphine-like substances that operate on specific receptor sites in the brain and spinal cord. These natural, internal opiates are called endorphins. Secreted and used by the brain, endorphins reduce the experience of pain and screen out unpleasant stimuli. In fact the presence of endorphins actually causes the feeling of well-being. . . . Behavioral researchers are learning that we can actually stimulate the production of endorphins through optimistic thoughts and a positive attitude.[4]

The bottom line for the speaker is this—people actually *feel better physically* after they have had a good laugh. The audience will be more relaxed and ready to receive your message after they have responded to a good anecdote.

Marilyn Elias, in an article in *USA Today*, cites corporate research showing that "underlings and women smile and laugh more than bosses and males."[5] This is important information for the speaker. When you do your audience analysis prior to planning your speech, and certainly before deciding on an appropriate rapport step for a specific group, realize that if you choose to use humor, it will be much harder to get a positive response out of a room full of men and/or CEOs.

I'm smiling right now, because when you add to this challenge the fact that I'm a *female* speaker, I have even more pressure to prove myself as an effective communicator within the first thirty seconds to a crowd like this. I must add, however, that once the group likes me and respects me for having excellent and worthwhile material that is presented in a confident manner, I'm home free! I thrive on challenges like this.

In the middle of this writing, I opened my mail. A couple of weeks ago I was speaking at a women's convention at the University of Waterloo in Ontario. There were seventeen hundred women in the audience, plus a couple of men who were in charge of recording the messages. One of the men just wrote to me and said, "Carol, thanks again for your A+ talks. I was one of the few males in the crowd, but I'm a pleased, challenged listener!" I used lots of humor at that conference, and it allowed me to get the attention of the audience so their hearts would be prepared to receive a very serious message.

I've spent a long time talking about the benefits of humor because it is an important vehicle in communication. Some of you are reading this, and red flags have been going up for the last five minutes. You're thinking, *But what if I'm not funny? I tell a joke, and no one ever laughs. I've tried humor on numerous occasions, and it doesn't seem to work for me. Does that mean I'll never be an outstanding speaker?* No!

Some of the most effective communicators I've ever heard do not have a God-given gift of humor. Several well-known Christian radio speakers rarely use humor, but their success as Bible teachers and/or inspirational speakers is widely known. If you are not funny, accept that fact and realize that there are many other techniques for effectively gaining rapport with your audience. The individuality of your personality will dictate the type of presentation that will make you "uniquely you" as a speaker.

There are many specific ways of gaining rapport. In the following examples, take time to study the transitional statement that ties the attention step into the main subject of the talk.

1. A Humorous Anecdote

A young lady named Cathy was thinking very hard one day when her mother walked into the room.

"Mom," said Cathy, "if I don't get married when I grow up, will I be an old maid like Aunt Elizabeth?"

"Yes, dear," said her mother.

"Well, Mom, if I do get married when I grow up, will I get a husband like Daddy?"

"Yes, dear," again came the reply.

After thinking this over for a while, Cathy put her hands on her hips and said, "Boy, Mom, we girls sure don't have much choice in life, do we?"

Transitional statement: I don't know how you feel about the choices you've made in life, but I do know that the choices I've made have ultimately determined everything about the quality of life I'm living today.

2. An Illustration Related to the Topic

A friend of mine, Deborah Jones, works on staff with Campus Crusade for Christ. She travels a great deal training and discipling other staff women who are working in campus ministries at major universities in a multistate area. Frequently, Debbie is asked to speak on current topics that will interest students in finding spiritual solutions to their key questions. One of the most popular talks is Deb's presentation titled "Understanding Men." Here's how she has adapted an old story to fit as a rapport step for a current message:

> As an eighteen-year-old college freshman, I knew what I wanted in a man. So, I began to look for my knight in shining armor on a white horse. At the beginning of my sophomore year, I realized that the color of the horse was not that important. When my junior year rolled around I thought, *Who needs armor? Besides, it just gets rusty!* As a senior in college with limited prospects, I decided to take the horse.

Transitional statement: Now I'm not recommending that you give up on men and go look for a horse. What I would like to do today is to share some of the building blocks and barriers that may help you better understand and develop healthy relationships with men.

3. A Series of Thought-Provoking Questions

If you're not a humorous speaker, here's your chance to bring in a touch of humor that will generate tremendous warmth—and you don't have to tell any jokes. Try these questions for opening a talk on time management or personal Christian discipline:

- How many of you have the problem of too much time on your hands?
- How many of you suffer from interruptions, commonly known as the pauses that don't refresh?
- How many of you have things to delegate and nobody to delegate to?
- How many of you think, honestly *think*, about losing weight?

If they aren't laughing by this time, they aren't in the land of the living! Note that you haven't had to work on key timing for a clever anecdote or on the punch line of a funny story—you've just asked well-worded questions. *Now* what do you do? Decide where you're headed. If you're going to talk about a disciplined devotional life, try this:

Now don't raise your hands on this one, but are you in the ranks of those who are convinced they will read the Bible all the way through this year, and once again you made it through Genesis, Exodus, and the first half of Leviticus before you quit and decided to wait on this project until next year?

Transitional statement: As Christians, we have a great need to spend time in the Word of God to get important instructions from our heavenly Father. Let's turn to Mark 1 and discover an action plan for ourselves as we analyze twenty-four hours in the life of Christ.

It's often possible to combine a question-style rapport step with humorous anecdotes. If I'm with a group for the first time and will be giving more than one talk, I often begin the opening session in this way.

How many of you are the parents of children ages five or under?
(Wait for hands to lift.) These are the parents who long for five minutes
alone in the bathroom. Mavis Trask, a dear friend and fellow speaker,
in years past had three children under school age. On one occasion
her two babies were asleep, and her four-year-old was outside playing,
so Mavis decided to take a bubble bath. She had just settled into the
tub when the bathroom door opened and in walked her son and five
preschool neighbors. They all gathered around the bathtub as her little
boy proudly announced, "And this is my mama!"

***How many of you are the parents of children from ages six
through twelve?*** These are some of the meanest parents in the world.
They say things like: "Did you finish your homework? Have you made
your bed? Are you through with your piano practice? You didn't feed
the dog!" I'm in the ranks of those of you in this category. It's a very
special time when children are asking deep questions and voicing curi-
osity about their world.

One day I looked at our eleven-year-old son, J.P., and said, "Jason,
do you know that when you grow up and get married, and when you
and your wife have children, I'm going to be a grandmother?"

He paused for a long minute and calmly said, "Mom, I don't know
if that's ever going to happen."

"Why is that, honey?" I questioned.

"I just don't know if I'll be able to find a godly woman," he
responded.

You'd better believe that I've written that statement down, and I'll
be reminding him of his priorities at a later date!

***How many of you are the parents of children from ages thirteen
through nineteen?*** These parents cry a great deal. Mark Twain offered
some advice to parents of teens: "When a child turns thirteen, he should
be put into a barrel and fed through a knothole." Twain continued:
"When the child turns sixteen, you should close up that hole!"

I realize that some of you are sailing through this period and your
children are your best friends, but some of the rest of you are struggling.

I'm sure all of us can agree that there are some easy seasons of life and some that are much more challenging.

How many of you are grandparents? Beatrice Bush Bixler, the beloved pianist-composer of several well-known songs, always shares a poem with her audiences. I don't know if it's original with Bea, but I first heard it from her and I'd like to dedicate it to you grandparents in the audience.

> My glasses fit me dandy,
> My false teeth fit just fine,
> My hearing aid comes in handy,
> But I sure do miss my mind!

Are there any single people in the audience? I'd like to welcome all of you. I heard a story about a young woman who was single a little longer than she wanted to be, and she decided to pray more specifically. She purchased a pair of men's trousers, just the right size, and hung them on the bedpost every night. She got on her knees and prayed, "Father in heaven, hear my prayer, and grant it if You can: I've hung a pair of trousers here; please fill them with a man." This woman married at the age of thirty-one and lived to raise twelve children. Some people get much more than they pray for!

Transitional statement: I may have missed your category. You may no longer have any children at home, and you're not a grandparent yet. Or perhaps you are married, but you do not have children. Some of you had your hands up in several categories. I want to say to all of you, "Welcome!" I believe that God has brought this unique combination of people together for His purpose this evening! We're here to discuss what the Bible says about family communication, and I'm sure there are vital principles in tonight's message that will benefit each one of us.

Because of the length, this grabber can be used only when you have a longer time to speak, but its effectiveness is hard to beat. It relaxes people and helps them identify with many others in the audience. In essence, it gives them a sense of community as they look around and realize that they are not the only ones who are dealing with the pressures of life.

There are other, much shorter, question-style rapport steps that can be used to introduce a talk. Ginger Sisson, a wonderful Bible teacher and frequent staff member with the Speak Up seminars, sometimes uses this opening after asking people to get out paper and pen:

- If you could change anything about your body, what would it be?
- If you could change anything about your immediate family, what would it be?
- If you could change anything about your finances, what would it be?

Transitional statement: Take a look at your answers to these questions, and you will discover the areas of your life where you lack contentment. Open your Bible to Philippians 4, and let's check out Paul's advice on how to experience God's contentment in the middle of difficult circumstances.

4. A Reference to the Music, Occasion, or Problem

There are certain times when it's better to make a brief opening comment and immediately get into the main thrust of your talk. I accepted an invitation to speak for a luncheon in the month of July, and I was told there would be a patriotic theme. After I was introduced, the emcee said, "But before Carol presents the message, we'll have the former Miss Florida present some patriotic music." As it turned out, Miss Florida was an exceptional musician, and by the time she ended with "The Battle Hymn of the Republic," the members of the audience were so motivated, they were ready to march in a parade. They didn't need my carefully prepared opening anecdote. It was much more appropriate to comment on the music, which was the perfect transition to my talk.

If you are addressing a group that once included you as a member and you haven't seen the people in a long time, or if you have strong denominational ties with them, it's always proper to greet them and identify your common bond. You generate warmth and instant respect because of your shared interest and/or affiliation.

When you accept an invitation to speak on behalf of an organization with a cause, get current statistics and use them in your opening. I was recently asked to speak for a fund-raising banquet for the March of Dimes. The best way to establish rapport with the group was to cite statistics on children born with birth defects and corresponding statistics on how many of these young people had been helped through the donations of concerned people like those in the audience.

5. An Interesting Description of Your Topic

Years ago I read a medical definition of the tongue. For some unknown reason the definition intrigued me enough that I memorized it. I have occasionally presented a message on the tongue, and I begin like this: Did you know that people in medicine say the tongue weighs about two ounces; it's about four inches long; and it's a slab of mucous membrane that wraps itself around an array of nerves and muscles and helps you to chew, to taste, and to talk!

Transitional statement: Obviously, the tongue can't do anything wrong by itself. It's simply the bucket that dips down into the well of your being. Jesus said in the gospel of Matthew that it isn't what goes into the man that defiles the man; it's what comes out of him. We're going to look at God's answer for dealing with the problem of the tongue.

I think people are utterly amazed that someone would actually memorize such an unusual definition, and the audience is listening intently at the end of my brief recitation.

6. A Startling Statement of Fact or Opinion

In an editorial in *Christianity Today*, a statistic jumped off the page:

When sports researcher Robert Goldman polled 198 world class athletes, he asked, "Would you take a pill that would guarantee a gold medal even if you knew it would kill you in five years?" More than half agreed they would.[6]

Transitional statement: What do you value most in life? Tonight we're going to talk about how to find lasting fulfillment.

This type of rapport building is especially useful when you have only a short time to speak. If you are given five to ten minutes for your presentation, you wouldn't want your opening illustration to last four minutes. The startling statement immediately gets people to think about your subject.

7. A Quotation

Will Rogers once said, "We are all ignorant; we are just ignorant about different things."

Transitional statement: I'm excited to be here because every one of you is an expert in something that I probably know very little about. I hope that I know more about communication than you do. Together, this weekend, we'll be learning from one another as we participate in lectures, discussions, and small-group activities.

Use a search engine to find quotations by topic on the Internet.

8. A Rhetorical Question

If you're like me, you've heard of rhetorical questions for years, but you haven't quite had the motivation to find out exactly what they are. According to *Webster's New World Dictionary*, a *rhetorical question* is "a question asked only for rhetorical effect, no answer being expected." Just what you thought, right?

Do you ever wonder who you really are? The post office lists you as "Occupant." The phone company says you are 555-0898. To the local bank you are 33-029-372. To the passerby you are 7890 on your street. Do you ever feel like a number? Like part of a smooth-running machine? Do you feel trapped in a world of computer printouts?

Transitional statement: According to the Bible, you were made for a very distinct purpose as a person of great worth and dignity. Have you ever considered the importance of discovering the real purpose of your existence on this earth? Today we're going to explore why the human race was created and how we can have a bright future and hope for tomorrow.

9. A List of Statistics

Current statistics demand the attention of your audience and immediately give you credibility. A speaker who reads the newspaper and stays up-to-date on vital new statistics recorded in periodicals or gathers recent data via the Internet will quickly gain the respect of an audience. But once again, be certain to cite them accurately.

As a Christian, I don't want to be like the ostrich who stuck his head in the sand, not realizing that the largest part of his anatomy was still showing. I desire to be informed, thinking, and current.

A few months ago I was speaking at a convention for educators and administrators. I left my hotel room, attaché case in hand, with my prepared talks for the day ready to go. On my way to the coffee shop I purchased a newspaper, and on the front page I read statistics from the Search Institute on why kids worry. In my opening remarks that day I held up the paper and said to several hundred teachers, "According to today's newspaper, in a poll of 8,000 children, ages 10 to 14, the number one reason why children worry is because of 'grades.' The top three reasons include grades (56 percent), looks (53 percent), and popularity (48 percent)."

Transitional statement: As educators, we must consider this vital information. Are we concerned only about teaching facts, or are we also concerned about meeting the emotional needs of children?

10. A Visual Aid

People will always remember your opening longer if you use a visual. I have a sign I purchased in a hardware store that has a black background with bright orange, glow-in-the-dark letters on it. It states simply, Wet Paint.

Occasionally, I have begun a talk by holding up that sign for all to see. After a momentary pause, I continue: My first reaction, after reading a sign like this, is to *touch* the surface to see if the paint is *really* wet.

Transitional statement: Have you ever had trouble believing that a statement is true? The Bible records that Jesus rose from the dead. Today we're going to take a look at evidence that backs up this statement. I challenge you to decide on the verdict for yourself!

This list is not the end of the available ways and means for getting the attention of your audience—it's the beginning! Evaluate the talent in your group. Do you have participants who are dramatic? Could you work with them to produce an opening drama that will introduce your topic? Perhaps someone could walk in from the back of the room in the costume of a biblical character and present a monologue that introduces the class to the culture of the day and the challenges that person encountered. By now your creativity is in full motion, and you've probably realized that your best method of deciding how to begin a talk is to ask yourself, *Who is in this audience?*

Remember these key points:

- Keep your opening brief if you have a short time to speak. A wise man once said, "After you get water, quit pumping."
- Choose your words carefully. You have thirty seconds to interest the audience in your talk before they start daydreaming.
- Plan your transitional statement carefully. It's the bridge into your main message.
- Be alert! Every day as you listen to the media or read newspapers and periodicals, clip, save, and write down ideas that could be developed into effective grabbers.

The goal of a rapport step is not to *charm* the audience into thinking you are Mr. or Mrs. or Miss Personality, but to successfully turn their attention to the subject at hand. Pray that God will give you insight into the very best method of capturing the attention of the group so that they will be listening to the important content in your message. You *can* start with a bang!

SIX

Finishing Touches

Preparing the Conclusion and Putting It All Together

Inspiration without perspiration leads to
frustration and stagnation.[1]

— DR. BILL BRIGHT

I am *motivated*! My engine is running, and I'm ready to set the world on fire! My husband and I have just returned from the annual meeting of the Million Dollar Round Table (MDRT) in Orlando, Florida.

The MDRT is the industry convention for people who work in the field of life insurance. The convention planners bring in the top motivational speakers in the country as well as outstanding musicians. Some of the finest multimedia presentations available are presented at these meetings. We were two of nine thousand participants from around the world — and the electricity was contagious!

Anyone wearing the official MDRT name tag could expect to be greeted enthusiastically by fellow members of this group just about anywhere — hotel lobbies, elevators, restaurants, Disney World or Epcot Center, even the attractions at Wet 'N' Wild! The members of this group like people — and whether or not they can make a living in the insurance business is determined by how much people like and trust them. My husband, Gene, is a member of this illustrious group.

The closing ceremonies were nothing short of an extravaganza. It was July 3, the day before Independence Day. The band struck up a chord, and singers marched onto the enormous stage in the convention hall. As they sang a medley of patriotic numbers, including "America the Beautiful," moving pictures appeared on two huge screens. The pictures were close-ups of immigrants coming into New York harbor; they were setting their eyes on the Statue of Liberty for the first time. Ellis Island was in sight, and they were almost touching the shoreline of a free country. Can you *feel* the emotion?

The grand finale included flags and fireworks—*inside* the building—and the chorus broke into a rousing rendition of "The Star-Spangled Banner." We all stood to our feet as a facsimile of the "Lady," complete with lighted torch, emerged from the electronically controlled stage.

Talk about a conclusion—it had it all! As we walked out into the sunshine and headed for the parking lot, echoes of the past few days could be heard everywhere.

"What a great convention!"

"God bless America!"

"I can't wait to get home and put these principles to work in my life and business!"

"We work in the best industry around, and we live in the most wonderful country in the world!"

A person could definitely suffer from overstimulation if given a steady diet of this type of programming, but for a one-time shot in the arm, it was spectacular! How wonderful it was to spend four days with energy givers instead of energy drainers. The ending summed up everything the speakers had said throughout the convention—*be* the best; *do* your best; *expect* the best; *give* your best! (Some of you, like me, might like to pursue an in-depth discussion of motivation, success, and the Scriptures, but that's not what this chapter is about. Too bad—it would have been a stimulating "rabbit trail," and I *love* a debate!)

EFFECTIVE CONCLUSIONS

The purpose of the conclusion of a speech is much the same as that of a convention. You want to focus the thought and feeling of the audience on the central theme that has been developed. What do you really want your listeners to take away with them? Do you want them to be challenged to take a specific course of action? Do you want them to believe in something? Did you simply want to inform them? Do you want them to be inspired?

Alan H. Monroe has this to say about a good ending:

> In addition to bringing the substance of the speech into final focus, a good ending should leave the audience in the proper mood. . . . Decide whether the response you seek requires a mood of serious determination or good-humored levity, of warm sympathy or cold anger, of thoughtful consideration or vigorous immediate action; then plan to end your speech in such a way as to create that mood. . . . The end of a speech should convey a sense of completeness and finality.[2]

There are several effective methods for ending a talk. Some that are most often used with excellent results include the following:

1. A Quotable Quote

If you have a short time to speak, a quotation works very well for conveying your main point. Be sure the quote embodies the central idea of your speech. If the author is familiar to the audience, the impact will be even greater.

In a message on why God allows suffering, I might say, "To sum up what we have studied today, I'd like for you to repeat a statement with me that I first heard from Stuart Briscoe. 'Things happen *to* me, so that things can happen *in* me, so that things can happen *through* me.' Please say that with me."

This particular quote has built-in gestures that make it even more powerful. "Things happen *to* me . . ." (hands flat on chest); ". . . so that things can happen *in* me . . ." (fingers pointing inward); ". . . so that things can happen *through* me" (palms open, hands outstretched toward the audience).

2. A Dynamic Challenge

This method is often used by ministers and motivational speakers. The speaker discusses the problem and makes positive suggestions for the solution. Then it's the listener's turn to do something. The wording of this challenge needs to be compelling, and the listener should understand the benefits of accepting the challenge when the speaker is finished.

Charles Swindoll ends one of his messages in this way:

Deterioration is never sudden. No garden "suddenly" over-grows with thorns. No church "suddenly" splits. . . . No marriage "suddenly" breaks down. No nation "suddenly" becomes a mediocre power. . . . Slowly, almost imperceptibly, certain things are accepted that were once rejected. Things once considered hurtful are now secretly tolerated. At the outset it appears harmless, perhaps even exciting, but the wedge it brings leaves a gap that grows wider as moral erosion joins hands with spiritual decay. The gap becomes a canyon. That "way which seems right" becomes, in fact, "the way of death." Solomon wrote that. He ought to know.

Take heed, you who stand: take heed, lest you fall! Be careful about changing your standard so that it corresponds with your desires. Be very cautious about becoming inflated with thoughts of your own importance. Be alert to the pitfalls of prosperity and success. Should God grant riches, fame, and success, don't run scared or feel guilty. Just stay balanced. Remember Solomon, who deteriorated from a humble man of wisdom to a vain fool in a rather brief span of time.[3]

3. A Plan of Action

An action plan often goes hand in hand with a challenge. The listener is encouraged to feel that a personal response is the vital ingredient. The desired outcome could be an internal decision such as accepting Jesus Christ as personal Savior. This type of appeal should be specific and should suggest an itemized course of action. It should include specific steps for completing a plan.

Example: Here's what you need to do to experience peace with God —

- Admit your need.
- Be willing to turn from your sin.
- Believe that Jesus Christ died for you on the cross and rose from the grave.
- Through prayer, invite Jesus Christ to come in and control your life, receiving Him as Lord and Savior.

4. A Thought-Provoking Question

You might ask a key question throughout your talk, and its repetition at the end of the message will cause the listener to make a choice. Another way to use the question technique is to close with an illustration followed by a personal question. Here is a good example:

In an art gallery there is a portrait of the great General Booth, with a radiant, glowing face, bent in prayer over an open Bible. One evening, as the janitor was closing that room for the day, and all the crowd had gone, he found an old man gazing at the picture with tears streaming down his face and saying over and over again, "Lord, do it again, do it again." Would you say that to Him now?[4]

5. A Summary of the Main Points

In *How to Say It Better*, William Hobby reminds us of a basic truth. He says,

> An old preacher explained, "First, I tell them what I am going to tell them.
> "Then, I tell them.
> "Finally, I tell them what I told them."[5]

It's true—in your final minutes before the group, you have one last opportunity to make your point, emphasize your aim, and tie the ends together. Summarizing the essence of your talk provides an excellent conclusion by reinforcing everything you've been saying all along. You simply repeat the main points of your outline with emphasis.

6. A Statement of Personal Intention

You may be asked to speak for a group that needs to raise money for a specific cause, or the group might need volunteers for a special ministry or activity. If your prestige with the audience is high, a statement of your own decision to take the recommended course of action is powerful. There may be members of the group who respect you enough to support the cause with money or time because you are going to do it, too.

As a speaker, take the necessary time to fully explain the need, and then build the conclusion around your own decision to do something tangible. Assuming a positive response is important here: "I know you, like me, have become aware of the problem . . . and you're wondering how you can help. Here's what I've done, and I know you will want to do the same."

7. A Key Story

A closing story can be a personal illustration or that of someone else. It can be current or historical. The important factor is that it contains the *kernel* of your main idea or that it suggests the action you wish the audience to accept. I'm always looking for a special story that will cause the audience to seriously consider my aim.

While I was in Indianapolis for a three-day seminar a couple of years ago, I was invited to stay in the home of Pam and Bill Mutz. What an incredible family! I was immediately impressed with the quality parenting these two were giving their three children—abundant, unconditional love combined with the right amount of discipline. Sitting at their table, first for dinner and then for family devotions, was an education in itself. Everyone participated—including the guest!

The next day I asked my hostess what made their Christian home so uniquely special. She began her story.

A few years earlier, when their older daughter, Cari, was just two and a half years old and their son, Jonathan, was seven months old, the children were in the bathtub together. That week Pam and Bill had out-of-town company, and the guest had brought two dogs with him that were left outside in the yard. While Pam was bathing her children, she became concerned that the dogs might get too far from the house.

Jonathan had been sitting up well on his own, and Pam turned to Cari and said, "Honey, please watch your brother for just a minute while Mama checks on those dogs."

Pam was gone a short time, but when she returned, Jonathan was under the water. Cari didn't realize the danger. Pam grabbed her son and screamed for the guest, who came down and did mouth-to-mouth resuscitation, while Pam called for an ambulance.

"They laid my Jonathan on a stretcher and worked feverishly over him, but even before we reached the hospital, I knew that he was gone," she said. In the days that followed, friends and family gathered, feeling Pam and Bill's grief as their very own.

I asked Pam about the long-term effect of this crisis point in their home. She said, "Carol, God has done an emotional and spiritual healing here that even psychologists do not understand. We know it's the Lord."

She continued, "Cari speaks often of her brother and looks forward to seeing him in heaven someday. Every time she gets a helium balloon, she rushes outside. Then she lets it go as she shouts into the heavens, 'Jesus, this is for Jonathan, and tell him it's from Cari!' I just know those balloons will make it—all the way! One day, perhaps Jonathan will greet us with an armful of balloons when we have the privilege of joining him in heaven!"

Two months after returning home, I opened my mail and enjoyed a wonderful letter from Pam. Enclosed with the note was this entry from her quiet-time notebook:

Jonathan,

Tell me, my son, what you are doing on this beautiful, heavenly spring day?

Are you romping through the tall fields of grass playing hide-and-seek with the other children in heaven?

Or are you sitting quietly by a babbling brook meditating on the miracles that God has accomplished in your young life?

Could you possibly be on kitchen assignment washing pans for the Master?

Or are you sitting at His feet praising God Almighty with your angelic voice?

Does our Lord tell you each time when we ask Him to communicate the precious "I love you's" and kisses we send?

Does He tell you how much we miss you and all the precious thoughts and words that Cari speaks of you?

Have you seen your new brother? Has God shown you his picture and told you all the stories of the cute things he has done? I know that they must make you chuckle! Jacob would love to play trucks with his big brother for hours on end!

Does Jesus tell you that we cry tears for you? You are our flesh and blood . . . our precious boy . . . at home with the best house-parent, Jesus.

But we miss you so much! Mom cries tears of longing

anticipation to once again hold her baby in the presence of our Jesus.

We love you, Jonathan. We love you very, very much.

Your Mom,
Pam

None of us knows when we, too, will face the most difficult test of our faith. Will you, like Pam and Bill, choose to trust God even if He never allows you to know *why* He has allowed a tragedy to enter your life? In the darkest hour of your days, God's one requirement is that you trust Him.

PREPARING THE CONCLUSION

Talking about technique after sharing this story with you is difficult. Obviously, the impact of a key illustration based on something that happened to you or someone you know personally is very powerful.

Timing is important, and a closing illustration of this length would require a sizable block of time to speak. Usually, the conclusion should be no longer than 5 percent of your total message. William Hobby states:

> Above all, be sure that your conclusion is forceful. Even while you are doing research and while you are writing the main body of your speech, you should keep your eyes open for material that you can use in making a dynamic conclusion. Spend whatever time it takes to word your conclusion effectively, then become so thoroughly familiar with it that you won't have to lose eye contact with your audience by referring to your notes.[6]

PRACTICING IMPORTANT GUIDELINES

Here are some guidelines to keep in mind:

- New concepts should not be introduced in your concluding remarks. Use this time to reinforce what you want the listeners to take away with them.
- Conclusions do not need to be long to be effective. Make your point and finish on time.
- Avoid false endings. When you say, "Finally" or "To summarize" or "In conclusion," and talk for another fifteen minutes, the audience can be annoyed.
- Write out, rehearse, and memorize the ending before trying it on the audience. This frees you to have excellent eye contact and to focus on the needs represented in the group at that time.
- Deliver your final sentence with confidence and finality—and then stop!

William E. Sangster has these words to say about this topic:

Having come to the end, stop. Do not cruise about looking for a spot to land, like some weary swimmer coming in from the sea and splashing about until he can find a shelving beach up which to walk. Come right in and land at once. Finish what you have to say and end at the same time. If the last phrase can have some quality of crisp memorableness, all the better, but do not grope even for that. Let your sermon have the quality that Charles Wesley coveted for his whole life: let the work and the course end together.[7]

No matter how carefully a conclusion is prepared, there will be times when something unusual occurs. You may be able to use this event or interruption to make an even more powerful ending than the one you planned.

A few years ago I was seated in the audience at Rodehaver Auditorium on the grounds of the great old Bible conference center at Winona Lake, Indiana. It was the final message of a three-day women's retreat. Millie Dienert was speaking, and her dynamic challenge from the Word of God was coming to a conclusion. Hearts were touched, and many in the audience wept as the Spirit of God brought conviction.

During her last few words before calling for a commitment, a woman near the front of the auditorium fainted. There was instant commotion as people cleared the aisle and tried to assist. Someone called an ambulance, and the crowd began to buzz.

"Did she have a heart attack?"

"Is there a nurse in the house?"

"What's happening? I can't see from here!"

Put yourself in Millie's shoes. What would you have done? As soon as it was apparent the situation was under control and the woman was receiving help, Millie had us bow our heads. She prayed earnestly for the physical needs of the woman — and then she prayed for us.

As she said, "Amen," heads lifted, and the sound of a siren could be heard. The ambulance attendants brought in a stretcher and carefully but quickly placed the woman on it. There was a hush in the room as we heard the vivid squeak of the wheels as the men rolled her out of the room.

Millie looked at us, paused for a moment, and, with penetrating eye contact and calm authority, said, "There may come a day when you, too, will be placed on a stretcher and carried out of a room. If on that day you meet your Maker, would you be ready?"

It was one of the most effective endings I've ever heard. Yes, Millie did a great job, but more than that, there were hundreds of people praying that the work of God would not be thwarted by the disturbance. The woman later regained consciousness and was perfectly okay, but in the meantime numerous life-changing decisions were made.

PUTTING IT ALL TOGETHER

The beginning chapters of this book have taught you how to prepare the individual parts of a talk, but how do you put it all together from start to finish? There are several essentials.

1. Pray for God's guidance and sensitivity to His Spirit.
2. Analyze your audience and the occasion.
3. Select your topic and narrow the subject.
4. Determine your aim. What is the *precise response* you are looking for from the listeners as a result of your speech?
5. Gather material. Become an expert on your topic by reading everything you can find on the subject. Interview people who could provide additional knowledge. Use dictionaries, commentaries, newspapers, magazines, and the Internet as additional sources.
6. Select the main ideas of your speech and arrange them in a clear, orderly fashion. Usually, this will be an outline with Roman numerals; however, you might use numbers or an acrostic, which we discussed in chapter 3.
7. Word the main body of the speech, filling in the structure by explaining or proving each of your points. This can be done with illustrations, facts, definitions, examples, figures, quotations, comparisons, and so on.
8. Write out your rapport step. Keep in mind that this step comes first in your speech, but it can't be planned until you know the content of your talk. (That's why "Start with a Bang!" is not the first chapter of this book.) The rapport step gains the attention of your audience and leads them into the subject of your talk.
9. Decide on the conclusion. What do you want the audience to leave with? If you don't know where you're landing, they won't, either!

10. Practice out loud. I know people who give messages to trees, mirrors, workbenches, car dashboards, and their relatives—and they improve! Record one of your practice sessions. Was your structure clear? How were the transitions? Do you need to delete some "uhms" and "ahs"? Could anything be told in fewer words? Should anything be added? Was your aim easy to identify, or was it too vague?

I hope you're excited! Since we are Christians, this is all God's work anyway. I do my part—pray, study, outline, select good illustrations, write out an aim that includes a specific action step, and choose a fitting introduction and conclusion. Then God does His part—and it's a winning combination.

If members of the Million Dollar Round Table left the stimulation of their annual meeting with all the fireworks and music and speakers and splash and went home and did nothing, they would not be successful long. The organization does its job of providing necessary information and wonderful inspiration, but no individual has ever become a consistent member of this group without practicing established principles and working very hard!

Likewise, God expects me to do my part in preparing for a message. Proverbs 19:2 says, "It is not good to have zeal without knowledge" (NIV). That remarkable inventor Thomas Edison once commented, "I never did anything worth doing by accident, nor did any of my inventions come by accident; they came by work!" On another occasion, he is credited with this important thought, true of speakers as well as inventors: "Genius is about 2 percent inspiration and 98 percent perspiration."

As a Christian speaker, I pray that God will pour His creativity into me as I prepare messages and place illustrations. While I'm praying, my eyes are open, and I'm alert to His great creation and resources. I work hard at careful preparation. The result? I reap what I sow! Try this advice recorded on a roadside sign in Kentucky: Pray for a Good Harvest, but Keep on Hoeing.

SAMPLE SPEECH

Now that we've covered all the elements of preparing a talk in these last four chapters, let me give you an example to show how it all works out in "real life." The following is a speech I've given many times. I'll lead you step by step through the preparation process and show you just how I put this talk together.

"Communication — Your Key to Success"

Rapport—gaining the attention of the audience and leading them into the subject of your talk. (The example shows use of a personal experience related to the topic. You are answering the nonverbal question of the listener, *Why should I listen to you?*)

Communication is often described as the key to a successful life, but what is it? I once asked a group of junior high school students to define communication, and they came through with astonishing insight. After pooling their ideas, they said:

> Communication is talking without a wall building up. It's hearing what was said and knowing what was meant. Sometimes it involves a look, or a touch, with no words at all. It's sharing in such a way that the other person really understands what you are saying. Listening is the hardest part of communicating.

If you have ever struggled in the area of communication, you have come to the right place. Today's topic is one that every person deals with. The quality of our relationships and our effectiveness on the job is largely determined by one thing — the quality of our communication skills. Communication *can* be your key to success!

Outline—the basic framework for your speech. (This is a keyword outline, using all nouns. Remember to keep the outline simple and memorable if your audience will be sitting at banquet tables without pen and paper in hand.)

- The Problem
- The Solution
- The Responsibility

Introduce the main body of your speech by giving an overview of your outline. "Today I'm here to remind you of the *problems* we face in communication, but my primary purpose is to present practical *solutions* and to challenge you to accept the *responsibility* of using your communication skills to produce positive change. You *can* make a difference!"

Illustrations and supportive material—filling in the outline with appropriate facts, subpoints, and illustrative material. Please note that when you are preparing your own notes, you may want to use a typical outline with your subpoints in Roman numerals. However, be sure the outline you place on the screen is not too detailed so your audience can easily assimilate your main points. It isn't possible to fully develop every illustration in the following example, but this outline will help you see how to put "substance" on the bare bones of the outline.

I. The Problem
   A. Communication *problems* are usually blamed on the "other" person.
      (Illustration—C. S. Lewis essay, "The Trouble with X")
   B. Communication *patterns* are hard to change.
      (Illustration—Have members of the audience cross their arms. Now have them cross their arms the other way. After they struggle for a moment, say, "Isn't change hard? Think with me. If it's this hard to change the way we cross our arms, changing the pattern of our well-established methods of communicating with others will take some work, too.")
   C. Communication *professionals* tell us important facts.
      1. Only 7 percent of our communication is expressed through the words we use.
      2. Thirty-eight percent of our communication is understood

through the tone of our voice.

3. Fifty-five percent of our communication is nonverbal and is more important than what we say.

Transition to next major point— "We've looked at the problem, but now it's time to focus on the solution. How can we develop better communication skills and encourage others to do the same?"

II. The Solution
   A. Recognize your need.
      (Illustration—"As a freshman university student in a very conservative school, I listened with amazement as my best friend told me of her encounter with the dean of women. Nancy had been caught holding hands with her boyfriend, and this behavior was strictly forbidden.

      "Responding to a summons, she was ushered into an office and came face to face with the dean. The well-meaning woman looked at my friend, paused a moment and, with deep sincerity, said, 'My dear girl, what are you saving for marriage?'

      "Nancy later reported that she had stifled the overwhelming impulse to stand up and say, 'The other hand, ma'am.'

      "When Nancy returned to the dormitory and shared her story, I determined at all costs I would learn how to communicate verbally, because tactile communication would get me into too much trouble. I had been *convinced* of my need!")
   B. Understand your purpose (see Genesis 2:18-24).
      1. God created us to enjoy companionship.
      2. God wants us to know completeness.
      3. The companionship and the completeness that God intended for us grow out of *communication*.
   C. Implement a plan.

1. Establish a personal relationship with Jesus Christ. (Determine if this audience needs to hear a gospel presentation.)
2. Make quality time with others a priority. (Give a personal illustration of overcommitment.)
3. Think first—then speak (see Proverbs 29:20). (Discuss the consequences of constant criticism. Quote an expert.)
4. Speak the truth in love (see Ephesians 4:15).
   a) Avoid an honesty-at-all-costs philosophy. ("I know this is going to hurt, but . . ."—see Ephesians 4:29.)
   b) Attack the problem, not the person. (Offer a personal illustration of a time when you blew it.)
5. Be an active listener (see James 1:19).
   a) Avoid interrupting or "tacking on."
   b) Ask questions that clarify.
   c) Restate the other person's content.

Transition to next major point—"We've defined the problem and talked about the solutions, but what is our responsibility?"

III. The Responsibility
   A. Choose to forgive (see Ephesians 4:32).
   Many of our worst communication problems come as a result of an unforgiving attitude toward others who have offended us.
   1. The most hurtful part of criticism is that there is often a small, infinitesimal amount of truth in it.
   2. If you *are* in the wrong, forgive and forget.
   3. If you are not in the wrong, forgive and forget anyway. (Share a key quotation or an illustration demonstrating the importance of forgiveness in restoring positive communication.)
   B. Communicate with God regularly (see James 5:16).

      1. Develop a meaningful prayer life.

      2. Make time for conversational prayer with others.

      3. Foster a spirit of praise and thanksgiving in your personal prayer time.

   C. Practice positive communication as a way of life.

      1. See the good in people and verbally affirm family members and coworkers. (Present a personal illustration of the positive result of this practice in your home or at work.)

      2. Think on things that are excellent and praiseworthy (see Philippians 4:8). (Give examples.)

Conclusion—your last chance to make your point, restate your main points, and tie it all together. The listener should be mentally asking: *What will I do about what I've just heard?* Your conclusion will be determined by who is in your audience. Do they need emphasis on communication with a personal Savior? Then use an illustration that will lead you to a gospel application. Do the group members need help with interpersonal communication? If they do, try something like this:

"As you've listened to this talk, you've probably been asking yourself, *What kind of communicator am I? Do I make the people who live and work around me feel comfortable or intimidated? Do I take the time to communicate with the people I say I care about the most? Do I have a healthy communication with God?*

"I'm reminded of the story about Jesus and a blind man (see Mark 8:22-25). The man came to Jesus and begged Him to touch him. Jesus took spittle and touched the man's eyes and asked him what he saw. The man tried to focus and said people looked like trees that were walking. Jesus touched him a second time and asked the same question. The man replied that he saw people as they really are.

"Sometimes we, too, see people as trees. Trees give us many things—wood, fruit, syrup, furniture, paper, and on and on—all things that are used for our utilitarian good. In our busy lives, we don't often mean to be people users or to be insensitive in our communications with others, but it happens. We need to follow the example of the blind man in Mark 8 and see people as they really are—with needs, hurts, and feelings. We, too, need a second touch from Him.

"Yes, in our society there is a communication *problem*, but you can be part of the *solution* by accepting the *responsibility* of establishing quality communication with the important people in your life. Communication is your key to success!"

PART THREE

How Do I Deliver a Talk?

SEVEN

Little Things Mean a Lot

Delivering a Message Effectively

"You heard my speech, professor. Do you think it would
improve my delivery if I followed the example of Demosthenes
and practiced with pebbles in my mouth?"
The professor smiled and said,
"I recommend quick-dry cement."

— BOB PHILLIPS

By now you have learned how to structure a talk on paper. What happens when you actually stand at a lectern in front of the microphone with a real live audience in front of you? Will they listen to what you have to say? Will they laugh at your jokes? Will they be disappointed? Will they be challenged? Will they ever ask you back? It all depends!

People can *talk* at the rate of two hundred words per minute, but people can *think* at the rate of thirteen hundred words per minute. Because the mind works so much faster than the speech mechanism, people in the audience can listen to your message and at the same time evaluate your appearance, eye contact, body language, and vocal variety.

Most people make a quick judgment. If your delivery captures their initial interest, you have the advantage. If not, they may mentally "leave the room" and not really hear what you have to say.

Psychologist Albert Mehrabian tells us what people *hear* when we speak:

- Seven percent involves the actual words we speak.
- Thirty-eight percent of the meaning is conveyed through our tone.
- Fifty-five percent of our communication is nonverbal and is more important than what we say.

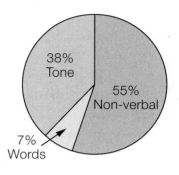

WORDS

Part 2 of this book taught you how to develop your manuscript content. But only 7 percent of the meaning derived from your speech will involve the actual words you speak. The only exception is when you are quoting the Word of God, which always has more power and application than normal speech.

TONE

Haddon Robinson says,

> Speech consists of more than words and sentences. The voice conveys ideas and feelings apart from words. We make judgments about a speaker's physical and emotional state — whether he is frightened, angry, fatigued, sick, happy, confident — based on the tremor of his voice, its loudness, rate, and pitch.[1]

Most of us received our first education in the importance of tone many years ago. Do you remember when your parents used to call you for dinner? My mom would call out the back door, "Carol, dinner is ready." If I didn't respond soon, the tone of her voice went higher, the volume increased, and she said urgently, "Carol, dinner is going to be served right away." If I lingered momentarily, I got the full-throttle yell—and my whole name! *"Carol Joy Afman, get in this house right now! This is the last call!"* I knew by Mother's *tone* that it was time to move.

Your voice is incredible! It works something like a wind or a stringed instrument; the vocal folds in the larynx vibrate in much the same way as the reed in a clarinet. Your vocal tone is actually produced by vibration of the folds as they are drawn together and as breath is forced between them.

> Voice begins . . . when a column of air is pumped from the lungs through the bronchial tubes, which connect the lungs to the windpipe. As the exhaled breath moves across the vocal folds in the larynx, located in the upper end of the windpipe, it sets up the vibrations that become sound waves. This sound is then amplified as it vibrates in the larynx, throat, sinuses and mouth. These . . . resonators act somewhat like the hollow section or soundboard of a stringed musical instrument, which increases the volume of sound made by the strings.[2]

Your resonators change shape when you move the jaws, teeth, palate, lips, tongue, and the back wall of the pharynx. These cavities actually produce the *quality* of your voice.

This may sound like a lot more anatomy than you care to know, but the bottom line is this: You can improve the quality of your vocal tone, without years of speech training, if you understand the importance of breathing and how to do it properly. Have you ever wondered how Jesus spoke powerfully to five hundred people without a microphone? He probably used diaphragmatic breathing.

As a speaker or a singer, you will be able to breathe more effectively if you involve the diaphragm. The diaphragm is a sheet of muscle attached to the sternum, the lower ribs, and the spinal column. This muscle should visibly expand when you inhale.

In lay terms, avoid using "upper chest breathing" for speaking, which causes your shoulders to go up and down. Instead use your diaphragm to fill your lungs with air; then say the alphabet in one breath and practice controlling your volume by varying how rapidly or slowly you contract the diaphragm. I also like to practice diaphragmatic breathing by repeating Scripture verses aloud. It is an aid to memorization *and* better vocal delivery.

Remember these key words about tone:

Volume

Use variation in loudness to create interest and emphasis. Whispering an occasional phrase can be more powerful than shouting it if you can be heard. On the other hand, it is very distressing to be in an audience and not *hear* the speaker. Ask someone to sit in the back of the meeting room to signal you if your voice is not loud enough. It is always helpful to meet with the sound technician ahead of time to test the microphone and amplification system. A former instructor of mine used to say, "Speak to the little deaf lady on the back row, and you'll be loud enough."

Variety

The movement of your voice up and down, like notes on a scale, is called pitch. Your general pitch will be determined by your own natural level. However, some of you may use too much of your "high" range, resulting in a voice that lacks authority. Conversely, if your voice is usually pitched too low, with little variance, you could sound overly strong and produce fear or subtle resistance in the audience. Use of no pitch changes at all results in a boring monotone. Strive to vary the pitch enough to communicate expressively the meaning of the words you are speaking.

Voice

This term has to do with the *quality* of sounds made in speaking. Listen to your voice on a video recording. Is it clear and crisp, or does it sound hoarse, breathy, or "fuzzy"? Can you hear the word endings? Be careful not to drop the *g* from *ing* in such words as *coming* or *going*.

Occasionally, I work with people who have a *lazy jaw*. They have never realized that they talk between closed teeth, which contributes to a nasal sound and a flat tone and seriously hurts the quality of vowel sounds. If you have this problem, my advice is to practice at home by opening your mouth more widely than normal to speak. Overpronounce your words, practicing precise diction. Use a recording to determine when your voice is easily intelligible. Clear, distinct diction makes listening easier.

Vibrancy

"Carol Afman—you're next!" It was the voice of my speech instructor in a mandatory freshman course. When I left home to pursue higher education, it never occurred to me that I would have to stand up in front of a room full of people and give speeches. I had no choice—Speech 101 was *required* for graduation.

I meekly left the security of my seat, mounted the dais, glanced at my carefully prepared notes, and began my speech. The opening sentences were barely out of my mouth when I heard the teacher say, "Young lady, you need more vitality!" Little did I know that by the end of that year the "desires of my heart" would change so drastically that I would become a speech major!

I learned the necessity of enthusiasm very quickly. If your voice has energy, warmth, and vibrancy, the audience will be anticipating what you have to say next. Some speakers have an excellent outline and meaningful illustrations, but the talk falls flat. Listen to recordings of your speech. Does your voice make the topic sound exciting? Is there any *energy* in your tone? Do you sound *alive*?

The Result

"Mom! Can you come *now*?" I was interrupted by our son, J.P., and his best friend, Christopher. The two boys led me to my kitchen, which had been turned into a sophisticated laboratory. All morning they worked on their latest invention, a highfalutin' solar energy system. They had painstakingly covered the inside of an old umbrella with heavy-duty aluminum foil using my last two rolls of tape.

The presentation began. With careful use of "the dramatic pause," the boys placed their impressive visual aid on the kitchen counter.

J.P. began, "This high-powered solar dish will be placed on our roof to collect energy from the sun that will be converted into electricity, which will travel down a wire into my bedroom window. All of the power needed for the electrical outlets in my room will be provided by our new energy system."

Chris chimed in, "We've never made an invention yet that failed!"

Their presentation had it all: *volume*—they were definitely loud enough; *variety*—I have rarely heard so many pitch changes in one short speech; *voice*—the boys' diction was clear and crisp so that every word could be heard; and *vibrancy*—it was off the charts! They were excited about their invention, they had faith that it would work, and they had me believing in it, too!

Did the invention work? Call me next year to discover the answer to this multiple-choice question.

☐ A. J.P.'s room is running on solar energy.
☐ B. We still pay a bill to the power company.
☐ C. Our house burned down.
☐ D. None of the above. J.P. is no longer interested in inventions; he likes girls.

NONVERBAL

More than half the meaning you convey is done without words or tone; it's nonverbal and is actually more important than what you say.

Facial Expression
Proverbs 15:13 says, "A joyful heart makes a cheerful face" (NASB). Do you scowl or frown when you're thinking? Relax and look for "friendly

eyes" out in the audience. Smile often and let your joyful face be an encouragement to a nervous retreat director or a frightened musician.

Kay Arthur is a dynamic Bible teacher and speaker. In one of her leadership training tapes she mentions that a woman new to her Bible study came up to her following the class and said, "Kay, why do you look so *mad* when you're teaching?"

Kay loves the Word of God, and her teaching style is aggressive and intense. It had never occurred to her that when she got fired up over certain passages of Scripture, her brow was furrowed, and her facial expression made her look angry. This observation encouraged Kay to relax her facial muscles so her face was communicating what her heart and words were expressing.

Ask a friend to give you feedback about your facial expression when you speak. Are you conveying a "mixed message," or is your face reinforcing what you really want to say?

Eye Contact

Eye contact is the most powerful form of nonverbal communication we have. In normal conversation people look at each other between 30 and 60 percent of the time. Michael Argyle states in his book *The Psychology of Interpersonal Behavior* that when two individuals look at each other *more* than 60 percent of the time while talking, they are probably more interested in each other than in what is being said.

Ralph Waldo Emerson once said, "The eyes of men converse as much as their tongues, with the advantage that the ocular dialect needs no dictionary, but is understood the world over." Many beginning speakers struggle with eye contact because it's very personal.

Eye contact invades another person's "space." When someone looks at you, you are forced to meet that gaze or to look away.

Eye contact is a powerful tool for the speaker. When you get up to speak, pause for a moment and look at the audience. Let your eyes move around the room, "connecting" with specific individuals.

During the course of your talk, include all sections of the

audience in your eye contact; it's easy to leave out the people in the balcony or those in your side vision. It's also tempting to look away from key individuals in an audience who may be experts in your subject area or people who are in some way threatening to you. Steady, controlled eye contact conveys your total confidence to the audience as a whole and to each individual.

As you speak, look at a specific individual for two or three seconds, and then move on to another person. Maintain eye contact long enough for the person to be aware of your actions. If the audience is large, do this with different sections of the auditorium. People sense that you are talking to them as individuals, not as a mass.

In *How to Read a Person Like a Book*, authors Gerard Nierenberg and Henry Calero say,

> Eye contact varies dramatically with different individuals. . . . Certain individuals, due to their shyness, tend to avoid eye contact or at least minimize it if at all possible. These persons could possibly be the most honest, sincere, and dedicated individuals around. However, every time they fail to look at the other person, they are unintentionally communicating doubt and possible prevarication.[3]

Okay, I admit it. I looked up *prevaricate* in the dictionary, and it means "to evade the truth" or "to lie." It's a fact; if you want people to believe your message, you must look them in the eyes!

For the speaker, eye contact conveys honesty and confidence, and it also provides you with feedback. You will observe subtle clues that tell you if the audience is understanding the message. A confused look indicates the need to give additional explanation or information. "Heavy eyelids" might convey fatigue. Pull out a good anecdote that fits the subject, especially if you're speaking after lunch. If too many people are looking toward the exit, finish your talk fast! Always quit talking before they finish listening.

Posture

At one of the Toronto Speak Up seminars, a young man approached me after the first evening and said, "Carol, I'm here because I need help. God has called me to preach, and I'm in my last year of seminary, but when I speak, no one responds. People don't seem to take my message seriously. What am I doing wrong?"

The next day I observed Tom carefully. His love for the Lord was obvious, and his desire to communicate God's truth challenged my heart. However, as Tom approached the lectern and began to speak, I soon realized that his shoulders were curved forward, which placed his hands awkwardly in front of him. He stood with most of his weight on one leg, causing his hip to tilt toward the left. As he read from the Scriptures, I received a mixed message. He was reading from the most important book in existence, but his body language conveyed weakness rather than strength.

Later, as we talked, I tried my favorite line as a speech coach: "Tom, if you could give this message again, what would you do differently?" Long ago I learned that most people already recognize their problem areas; if they bring up their own flaws first, it's easier to give suggestions for improvement without sounding too bossy. He looked at me with sincerity and said, "I honestly don't know." (I can hardly wait to hear from my editor: "Carol, if you could write this book again, what would you do differently?")

During the next two days, we worked on the problem. I demonstrated his visible body language and had him practice good posture—shoulders held back with the arms and hands hanging comfortably at his sides ready to gesture at the appropriate time. He worked on spreading his weight evenly on both feet, avoiding military stiffness, but conveying an authority that he had never demonstrated before. Then he presented the same speech—this time with powerful results. The only thing that had changed was his posture.

Watch a video of one of your presentations and evaluate your body language. Sometimes posture is improved if you imagine a make-believe string is pulling your head up and keeping your back straight. Improved posture will always add strength and authority to your message.

Body Language

In his book *Body Language*, Julius Fast says, "Body language can include any non-reflexive or reflexive movement of a part, or all of the body, used by a person to communicate an emotional message to the outside world."[4] Facial expression, eye contact, and posture are all parts of the whole when it comes to important ways the audience "reads" a speaker, but there are a few other things that must be considered.

Avoid leaning on the lectern except for brief periods of "getting intimate" with your audience. It's appropriate to touch the sides of the lectern, but avoid gripping it too hard—white knuckles definitely convey your nervousness and inexperience to observers.

As you become more comfortable with public speaking, move away from the lectern and give an illustration or a major section of your talk without a physical barrier between you and the audience.

You will be amazed at the results! The warmth of the audience is multiplied when they feel physically closer to you.

When you sit on a platform, sit tall. Slouching gives you a sloppy look and can even make you look heavier. (That's strong motivation for sitting up straight!) When seated on a platform in a street-length skirt, women should cross their legs at the ankle, rather than at the knee. From the front row more can be seen on the podium than you might think.

To prevent nervous mannerisms, such as rattling change in your pockets, fidgeting with a pen, or rearranging notes at the last minute, eliminate the causes. Empty all pockets of loose change, don't take a pen to the lectern, and have your notes in order *before* you arrive. From the moment the program begins, fix your attention on the person up front. Others are aware that you are the speaker, and your example will provide a powerful example.

Gestures

A gesture is the movement of any part of the body to convey a thought or emotion or to reinforce something you say. Gestures give added emphasis and vitality to your words and concepts.

Beginning speakers often struggle with gestures. They sometimes revert to clasping their hands behind their backs or clutching palms or fingers together in front of them, conveying an uncomfortable look. Subliminally, they must think that the hands will do something embarrassing if they are free to respond on their own. In my many years of training speakers, I have found that the hands and arms will do only what the brain tells them to do! Trust them!

Alan Monroe comments on the importance of gestures:

> The value of . . . gestures is threefold: they increase the speaker's energy and self-confidence; they assist in the communication of his ideas; and they help hold the audience's attention. By providing an outlet for his pent-up energy, gestures tend to relieve the muscle tension in the nervous speaker. To the lethargic speaker . . . the use of vigorous gestures is stimulating, quickening his pulse and making him more lively and animated.[5]

Let your gestures come naturally from *within*. A few years ago, a highly promoted women's musical group provided special music for one of our church services. They arrived in their stunning look-alike outfits, and at the proper time, they mounted the platform to sing their first number.

Following the musical introduction, the three of them, in unison, placed their eyes on the left side of the crowd and sang, "Heaven came down and glory filled my soul." In perfectly choreographed precision, their heads bobbed up, and their eye contact landed in the center of the auditorium on cue as they sang, "When at the cross the Savior made me whole." Without missing a beat, together the three heads looked to the right as the women belted out, "My sins were washed away and my night was turned to day when . . ." — back to center — ". . . heaven came down and glory filled my soul."[6]

In spite of my appreciation for John W. Peterson's much-loved song, it was one of the most humorous presentations I have ever observed. People in the audience were stifling laughter because the rehearsed gestures of the trio had turned a serious song into something else. It was an awkward moment, and no one knew how to respond.

The stroke of the gesture should fall exactly on, or slightly before, the point it emphasizes. If the timing is off and the gesture comes late, it looks "canned." Clowns use late gestures to get laughs. As speakers and/or musicians, we want people to laugh *with* us, not *at* us!

When you gesture, keep the upper arm an inch or two away from your torso, and make most hand gestures above the waist. This makes you appear more relaxed.

The size of your gestures should be in direct proportion to the size of the audience. In other words, the larger the audience, the larger the gesture should be to look natural and appropriate. In a huge convention center I would use wide, sweeping arm gestures; however, in a smaller room, the same gestures would make me appear arrogant, ruining my effectiveness as a speaker. Be aware of venues where a camera is projecting your image onto a gigantic screen. In this case, even if you are speaking in a large arena or auditorium, your gestures need to come in closer to your body or you will appear to be invading the intimate space of your audience.

If you're wondering how to deliver a message with appropriate gestures, there's one answer — practice, practice, practice until they feel natural. When you are comfortable, the audience won't be consciously aware of how dynamic your body language is. They will simply tell everyone that they loved your presentation!

Handshakes

The most powerful nonverbal communication we have is eye contact, but second on the list is the handshake. The way you shake hands says volumes about you. It will immediately tell someone if you are eager and confident or shy and unsure of yourself.

Nierenberg and Calero comment:

> The modern handshake is a gesture of welcome: the palms interlocking signify openness and the touching signifies oneness. . . . Many people consider themselves experts in analyzing character and attitude from a handshake, probably because perspiring palms usually indicate nervousness.[7]

The "dead fish" handshake conveys lack of interest and/or low self-esteem.

Practice a good handshake. Grasp the whole hand firmly, confidently look people in the eyes, and let them know you are genuinely happy to meet them. A weak, halfhearted handshake makes people feel unimportant and unimpressed. Remember—you represent the King of kings!

A CLOSING THOUGHT

A few years ago while I was reading the Gospels, I discovered two significant repetitions of body language by the Lord Jesus Christ. Scripture records repeatedly that "He looked with eyes of compassion" (see Matthew 9:36; 14:14; Luke 7:13), and "He touched them" (see Matthew 17:7; 20:34; Mark 1:41).

Communications experts now say that to feel loved and accepted, the average person needs twelve touches a day. A touch can be a hug, an embrace from a family member or friend, a squeeze on the arm from a coworker, or a slight brushing of shoulders with someone passed on a street or in a hallway. Physically touching someone makes us feel significant. Studies have been done in elementary school classrooms regarding the role played by the *touch* of a teacher, and the findings are not surprising. On the whole, students are higher achievers if a teacher tousles their hair or gives them a caring arm squeeze on a regular basis.

The important point is simply this—Jesus knew the secret. People need *eye contact* and *touch*. If we are to be discreet in this day and age, however, we would do well to practice warm, direct eye contact and a healthy handshake.

We should heed Luke 6:40 (NLT): "Students are not greater than their teacher. But the student who is fully trained will become like the teacher." As I study the life of Christ, the Master Teacher, my prayer is this: "Lord, give me eyes of compassion to *see* people the way You see them; help me to look beneath the surface and *touch* them with warmth, truth, and sincerity."

EIGHT

Pursue Excellence

More Tips for Speakers and Leaders

*Some people have greatness thrust upon them. Very few have
excellence thrust upon them. . . . They achieve it. They do not
achieve it unwittingly by doing what comes naturally and they
don't stumble into it in the course of amusing themselves. All
excellence involves discipline and tenacity of purpose.*[1]

— JOHN W. GARDNER

verage — I never liked that word. It reminds me of high
school — struggling to fit in, striving to have the right clothes or the
right "look," hoping to look intelligent, but not too intelligent. Do you
remember those days?

Dr. Layne Longfellow, research psychologist and professional speaker,
has done an intriguing study. He states that most people who were *jocks* in
high school turn out to be rather average in adulthood. Individuals who
were teenage *nerds*, however, have greatly enhanced chances of success.
It seems that the nerds have had to work so hard for so long to fit in that
they develop a "success mode" and become the real achievers in life.

WINGERS AND PLODDERS

There is hope for you and me! As I present the Speak Up seminars in
cities all over the country, I find a recurring phenomenon. The person
who was born with above-average ability in public speaking has often

developed a pattern of "winging it." For years this person has gotten by on a quick wit, a ready smile, a dynamic personality, and poorly prepared material. In high school, this individual could easily be elected to a class office on the wave of mere popularity. In college, it was a little tougher to maintain momentum, but a flash of that winning smile and a burst of enthusiasm went a long way. Upon reaching adulthood, the *winger* often lands a top position earlier than his or her struggling peers and gets by rather well with great natural ability.

For the majority of you who bought this book because you do not have an extraordinary gift in speaking and readily admit that it takes "blood, sweat, and tears" for you to make it through the preparation and delivery of a talk, there is good news. The *plodders* usually win in the long run.

Give me a plodder over a winger any day. I believe God's most important work is done by plodders who rely on Him instead of their own education, sense of humor, and strong natural leadership skills. Plodders know they need help and readily ask for it. They research their subject until they know everything about it. Plodders use marvelous visual aids because they prepare ahead of time instead of pulling things together the night before the speaking engagement. Plodders practice their speeches and rework outlines and illustrations.

Plodders pray a lot because they're scared to death. God honors hard work and prayer, and the unsurprising result is the genuine effectiveness and continuous growth of individuals who keep striving for excellence. The apostle Paul said, "And my speech and my preaching were not with persuasive words of human wisdom, but in demonstration of the Spirit and of power, that your faith should not be in the wisdom of men but in the power of God" (1 Corinthians 2:4-5).

A word to the winger—if you are blessed with a God-given gift for speaking, you have a choice. You could get by ad-libbing your way through your teaching and speaking opportunities for the rest of your life. The audience would still like you; they might even invite you back. Or you could choose to continue learning, stretching your mind with every new assignment, not relying on outdated illustrations and outlines as your only source of speaking material. The choice is up to you.

One final note is obvious. As the years go by, plodders finally catch up to wingers and eventually take the lead. I know of few audiences who would choose a steady diet of flashy splash over the prepared plodder. Plodders never become wingers—they surpass them! People who practice winning formulas make progress. When they try and fail, they get up and try again. And so, my fellow plodders, let's get on with it! What else do you need to know?

HOW CAN YOU OVERCOME STAGE FRIGHT?

You are standing in front of a packed auditorium, and your reputation is on the line. The introduction is over, and it's time for your speech to begin. The adrenal glands are shooting energy throughout your body, causing sweaty palms and a faster and faster heartbeat. Your breath is short, and your mouth is dry. Your hands are trembling. What could be worse? You can't remember anything—your mind seems to have stopped functioning.

You are not alone! It is estimated that 80 percent of the population suffers from stage fright. Although it is somewhat comforting to know there are fellow strugglers, what can you do about it?

Be prepared. One of the things that makes the Speak Up seminar unique is that participants get to try out what they learn. Many people register, thinking they will listen to the lectures and "pass" on doing the assignments. In most cases, I find that when people know what is expected of them and they have time to organize their thoughts through careful preparation, much of the panic connected with speaking is alleviated. It's when people stand up to speak and have nothing to say that terror overcomes them.

Be an expert on your topic. Read! Read! Read! When you know more about the subject than your audience does, you have the winning edge. If you happen to get a question from someone in the audience and you don't know the answer, admit it—with humor and a smile. A simple "I don't know, but I'll find out and get back to you" works well, also.

Focus on slow, rhythmic breathing before you begin to speak. Relax! Pause before your opening sentence, smile, and make eye contact with your audience.

Have a glass of water nearby. Beginning speakers often struggle with a dry mouth.

Practice positive body language and eye contact. This was discussed in the last chapter. When you *look* more confident, you feel more confident.

Rehearse in front of a mirror. This allows you to view your gestures, posture, and facial expression. Make necessary changes. Or better yet, videotape yourself and critique your performance.

Enroll in a public speaking course. There's no substitute for practice and instruction. If that's not possible, ask a friend to listen to your speech and give honest feedback.

Be positive. Ask yourself what the worst possible scenario could be. You could forget everything and sit down. The audience could walk out, or worse yet, they could *stay* and laugh at you. When all is said and done, the worst thing that could happen is a short-lived awkward moment of human suffering. But at least you tried!

Prepare for next time. Occasionally, a beginning speaker will conclude a talk, get back to a seat or even all the way home, and be hit with a rush of emotion—even tears. The overwhelming thought is that you've blown it and did a terrible job, when in reality your speech was very good, but your body is letting loose after intense stage fright. This doesn't happen to every first-time speaker, but it happens often enough that you should know you're normal. Try again. Move on to the next opportunity. Stage fright *feels* much worse than it *looks*.

How sad it would be to go through life with great amounts of wisdom and knowledge that you were afraid to communicate to others. If you try and fail, get up and try again. Failure is never final to the person who wants to improve and is willing to keep working. Plodders, keep on plodding!

HOW SHOULD YOU PREPARE AND USE NOTES?

I have used various techniques to prepare and use notes for speeches, but the ones I include here seem to be the most helpful. You may find that these techniques suggest others even more suitable for you as your style of speaking evolves.

The length of the talk will dictate the size of the notes. For a short talk, use sticky notes in your Bible or three-by-five-inch cards; for a longer presentation, use standard sheets of paper.

Make an outline of your talk. If you are a beginning speaker, write out your speech in manuscript form so that you can delete redundancies and choose the best wording for key illustrations. Wingers find this technique difficult but rewarding since it helps to eliminate their usual wordiness. Practice out loud from the manuscript a few times.

Work to reduce your notes. Move from practicing with the manuscript to a sentence outline of the body of the talk. Use bullet points, numbered points, or Roman numerals.

Memorize your opening and your conclusion. This allows you to have excellent eye contact with the audience during two crucial times in a speech.

Avoid memorizing your entire talk or reading from the manuscript. Use your outline for the actual talk. If you've done your homework, you will sound knowledgeable and spontaneous, not academic and boring.

Highlight or circle main points or key words. You can do this with a translucent marker or felt-tip pen of a bright color (I like red). If you lose your train of thought, a quick glance will put you back on track. A highlighter will work, too, but I prefer a fine-tip marker since I can write with it.

Reduce your notes from a sentence outline to a key-word outline. This is especially appropriate if the speech is one you will present in different places on numerous occasions.

Use as few cards or pages as possible. If people in the audience see a whole bundle of notes, they wonder how long you plan to talk.

Number your note cards or pages. Occasionally, notes are misplaced or dropped and need to be reshuffled fast!

Use only one side of the paper for your notes. Practice sliding the pages over as you finish each one rather than stacking them under the unused sheets. It's too easy to mix up the order and lose your place.

Avoid folding your notes. They never seem to lie perfectly flat after that and can become an eyesore to the audience besides being difficult for you to see.

Use loose pages for your notes. The use of a ring binder for notes is debatable. I find the flipping of pages in a notebook or over the top of a legal pad distracting. It's also easy to hit the microphone as a page is being turned. However, the beginning speaker often finds security in a binder where notes will stay in perfect order and rest securely on the lectern until the next page is turned. If this enhances your "comfort zone," by all means use a binder—for a while, but not forever!

Check the lectern. Some do not have a "lip," and notes can slide off. If necessary, ask for an orchestra stand; these stands are mobile, adjust easily to any height, and hold a lot of weight.

Use your notes. Notes are not a sign of weakness; they are a sign of careful preparation. Don't apologize for notes, but use them discreetly. In truth, I am the most confident and do a more competent job as a speaker when I know my material well enough to present it without notes—but every one of my best talks started with carefully prepared notes. Meticulous preparation is essential. Wingers, take heed! The plodders do their research well—and they are catching up fast.

HOW SHOULD YOU LOOK AS A SPEAKER?

The moment you enter a room you are making an appearance. You never have a second chance to make a good first impression. Have you heard these statements before? We have been inundated with books, videos, and seminars by color analysts, wardrobe consultants, body builders, nutrition experts, and diet gurus.

Among Christians there are two extremes. Some of you have bought the whole package—you look terrific and you're proud of it. Proper nutrition and exercise combined with up-to-date, well-fitting clothes have given you a sense of unequaled self-esteem. Some of you are fed up with the whole thing. You feel people have become slaves to their bodies and are caught up in outward appearance instead of inner beauty. The Bible *does* say, "What matters is not your outer appearance —the styling of your hair, the jewelry you wear, the cut of your clothes—but your inner disposition. Cultivate inner beauty, the gentle, gracious kind that God delights in" (1 Peter 3:3-4, MSG).

Where is the proper balance? How should a speaker look? Is good grooming essential? Is outward appearance important? Haddon Robinson says,

> When the apostle Paul declared that he would "become all things to all men, that I might by all means save some" (1 Corinthians 9:22, NKJB), he established a basic tenet of Christian communication. In matters of moral indifference, what matters most is not my feelings but the feelings and attitudes of others. Since grooming and dress make a difference in how a listener responds to us, they should make a difference to us.[2]

There are other important reasons for working on improving our physical appearance. We are the representatives of the Lord Jesus Christ on this earth. When I dress too hurriedly and throw myself together without care for important details, my mind is on myself. I wonder if the audience can tell my jacket isn't pressed. Did they notice the lint on my slacks? Can they tell my hair needs attention? The focus is me-centered instead of other-centered. I lack confidence because my self-esteem is lower, and the usual energy in my delivery falters. Not taking enough time for personal appearance can affect the quality of my entire presentation—and my whole day! I am able to do my best for Him only when I am not worried about what I look like and can concentrate on ministry. Proper preparation frees me to forget myself and lets me focus on other people.

Your selection of clothing for speaking will be determined by the *audience*, the *occasion*, and your own personal *style*. Absolute rules on dress are impossible because of changing fashions and hairdos, as well as different climates. But there are some appearance guidelines that do not fluctuate with our whims and times. John T. Molloy, author of *Dress for Success*, has been a wardrobe consultant to many of America's top corporate executives. He says,

> I am frequently asked if there are any traits common to all successful executives. There most definitely are; they always have their hair combed and their shoes shined. And they expect the same of other men, particularly subordinates. If your hair is disheveled, even if it is short, it triggers very strong negative reactions from other men.[3]

I believe the same holds true for women, and it's a great reminder for all speakers. However, be sensitive to the times. Currently, a moussed, disheveled hair style on a young adult man is considered avant-garde, especially if you are communicating to youth. If you aren't sure whether or not your appearance is adding or subtracting from the effectiveness of your presentation, ask a trusted colleague—and then prayerfully make the decision that feels right, based on who is in your usual audience.

The problem of being overweight as a Christian speaker is always a delicate one. People cite health problems and genetic reasons for weight retention—both of which give some individuals a lifetime battle with the scale.

It is difficult for an audience to hear someone who is forty pounds overweight speak on self-control. The heavyset speaker who says that God can do anything appears to be a living paradox. Often people blame others' culinary expertise for making them heavy instead of taking responsibility for their own lack of willpower.

The quality of ministry will improve when your weight is on target. A regular program of proper diet and exercise will give you more energy and confidence; your clothes will fit better; your blood pressure will be under control; you won't have to make unfunny jokes or apologies about your weight. You'll be representing the King with the dignity He deserves. Remember, He lives in you!

This was a difficult subject for me to discuss. I know some of you won't like me for mentioning it, and I take rejection hard. If you're struggling, ask yourself why. Do you need to set some realistic physical goals so that you can minister more effectively?

WHAT ARE SPECIFIC GUIDELINES FOR PLATFORM APPEARANCE?

Know something about your audience. Is there anything about your appearance that would keep the group from hearing what you have to say?

Several years ago I was invited to speak for a church women's meeting. Upon my arrival, I discovered that the women wore no makeup, and they were all dressed in navy blue or black. There was no jewelry in sight—not even wedding rings. There I stood in my rose-colored suit, lipstick, and jewelry. I was welcomed warmly, and the chairwoman ushered me to a seat. *Awkwardness* is not an intense enough word to describe what I was feeling. Would this group listen to a speaker who looked like I did that night?

During the preliminaries, all heads were bowed for prayer. I took a tissue and quickly wiped off my lipstick. Next I pulled off my rings, necklace, and earrings and dumped them into my purse. I couldn't do anything about the bright-colored suit, though.

The women were gracious, but I could have saved myself embarrassment and removed some barriers if I had obtained more information about the group before I arrived. I was not there to reeducate them regarding their liberty in Christ; my job was to teach the Word of God.

Find out what colors look best on you, and build a "speaking outfit" or wardrobe around those colors. Every individual has certain colors that make him or her look more healthy and dynamic. There are many excellent books on wardrobe and color, or you may prefer to make an appointment with a professional consultant.

Dress appropriately for the occasion. Find out what members of the audience will be wearing. Sometimes just knowing the location can give you a clue. Are you speaking in the ballroom of the Hyatt Regency or in the dining hall at a camp? It's always fitting for you to be dressed a bit more formally than your listeners. It's a way of honoring them and showing your respect for them.

Stand in front of a full-length mirror before leaving for your speaking engagement. Is your outfit well pressed? Are your shoes in need of new heels? Would you like to look at *you* for an hour?

Tips for Women Speakers

1. Avoid the "sleeveless" look. A jacket and skirt or dressy pants are always in good taste, and classic design in your clothing brings added authority to your message. If you live in a warm climate, jackets may not always be practical. A dress would be suitable, but be sure that the dress is not cute, floral, or striped.

2. For a stylish "together" look, bring the color worn below the waist to the top of your body. (For example, if you're wearing navy blue pants and a white blouse, a navy scarf, silk flower, or pin would bring a more coordinated look to the outfit.)

3. Stay away from tight-fitting clothes, see-through materials, daring skirt slits, and anything that might call attention to you rather than to your message.

4. Be conservative with jewelry. Avoid bangle bracelets or anything that might hit the microphone or lectern.

5. Makeup should bring your face to life, but not look "heavy." Most makeup companies will give one free facial and will teach you how to apply makeup properly.

6. Wear nail polish only if you have attractive nails. Also, no nail polish is better than chipped polish.

7. Take a look at your hair. Is the style up-to-date? Do you need a cut or a trim?

8. Learn to use accessories — they help you get a lot of mileage out of one suit in a basic color. The popularity of certain kinds of accessories changes regularly, but ask a friend who has a good sense of style to give you advice about appropriate accessories to complete your outfit.

9. Wear stylish but comfortable shoes. If your feet hurt, it will show in your voice. Closed-toe and closed-heel shoes suggest "business" rather than "fun."

10. Use common sense. As you look in the mirror, honestly evaluate if there is anything about your appearance that might take away from your ability to communicate to your audience. If something is in question, eliminate it.

Tips for Men Speakers

1. A solid-color suit in a wool or wool-blend is best for authority and versatility. The wool-blend is best for travel since it will not wrinkle as easily as the all-natural fabric.

2. Your shirt and suit need to contrast, but the suit and tie need to be darker than your shirt. The more color contrast between shirt and suit, the more authoritative the look.

3. Silk or silk-blend ties are the most attractive.

4. Ties should always be long enough to touch the top of the belt, but they can be worn longer. The suggested length of ties varies with changing times. Ask a trusted colleague or friend to give you advice.

5. Black socks are appropriate with all dark shoes. Wear only camel or tan socks with camel or tan shoes. Reserve white socks for athletic attire.

6. Eliminate extremes in your choice of accessories. Gold jewelry and gold pens give a quality look.

7. Have your hair cut and styled regularly.

8. Shoes should be polished, and the heels should be in good shape, not in need of repair. If you live in the North, protect your shoes from salt stains.

9. Pockets should not bulge with a collection of pens, keys, handheld electronics, cell phones, glasses, loose change, and a wallet.

10. Suits and shirts should be spotlessly clean and pressed.

Appearance *does* matter. In Amarillo, Texas, a woman came up to me at a conference and said, "I came because I liked your picture in the brochure. You have a businesslike, attractive appearance, and I thought you might have something worthwhile to say." She certainly made my day, but the important point is this: Non-Christians will first be attracted to *you*, before they are attracted to your message. You are an instrument, not an ornament!

WHAT ARE TIPS FOR USING A MICROPHONE PROPERLY?

Microphones are a lot like people—no two are exactly alike. That's not quite true, but it does establish an important point. The size and the quality of sound equipment vary dramatically; whenever you can test a microphone before the audience arrives, do so. That luxury is not always available, so here are some hints.

Adjust the height of the mike so it is aimed at your mouth, about six to eight inches away from you. Never hunch over a microphone to reach down to the mouthpiece.

Test a microphone by speaking into it normally. Never blow into it. Have a friend signal you from the back of the room to indicate if you are loud enough.

Request an over-the-ear or a clip-on microphone if you like to move around when speaking. It frees your hands to gesture. When clip-ons are not available, remove the microphone from the stand if you desire to stand in front of the lectern to get closer to the audience. It should be held six to eight inches from your mouth.

For question-and-answer sessions, don't aim the mike at the questioner. Instead, repeat the question yourself. This not only allows everyone to hear clearly, but you have an extra moment to consider your answer. (Those extra seconds can be very valuable to you!)

If the microphone whistles, the volume could be too high, the mike might be too close to your mouth, or you could be standing in front of one of the speakers.

Avoid shouting into the mike. Speak distinctly in your normal range. To emphasize a point by speaking more loudly, back away from the mike. If you lower your voice, lean closer.

Microphones magnify sound—make sure it's your voice that's being amplified, not rattling papers, coins, or clunking jewelry.

If you can be heard comfortably by everyone in the room, don't use a microphone. How large is the room? How big is the crowd? Using sound equipment for only a few people will make you seem to be striving for superiority. When the size of the crowd necessitates its use, the microphone can be an invaluable tool. Use it wisely; use it well.

HOW CAN YOU GET THE AUDIENCE INVOLVED?

You're speaking for a weekend conference. The participants arrived yesterday afternoon, checked into the hotel, came to the Friday night meeting, and then stayed up half the night talking. Saturday morning breakfast was at 7:30 a.m., and the schedule took them to a main session and to two workshops before lunch. A heavy noon meal was enjoyed by all since the conference committee knows the group likes to eat. It's now early afternoon, and you're up to speak. People are exhausted and ready for an afternoon nap. What can you do?

The amount of audience involvement you feel comfortable with will be determined by your personality and speaking style. I love to get people to participate. We live in a hurry-up world, and a large percentage of people in every audience are tired, so anything I can do to involve them in my presentation will be helpful. I've included here some of the methods I've found to be successful.

Use visual aids and technology—data projectors, video clips, pictures, flip charts, or a chalkboard. Visual stimulation will keep them alert. Be sure you prepare neat copy ahead of time, unless you will be drawing diagrams and writing down key points as you speak. When you use PowerPoint, don't reveal your entire outline at the beginning of your presentation. Reveal individual points as you teach them. When people see the whole thing at once, they usually copy it immediately and sometimes mentally tune out what you are saying until they are through writing.

Pass out printed copies of your outline, and have participants fill in the subheadings as you lecture.

Move away from the lectern and stand closer to the audience. I sometimes walk into the audience at a seminar and talk to one person—over the mike so all people can hear. This not only wakes people up—it produces tremendous intimacy between you and them.

Move muscle mass. If you are the last speaker after a long day, you might have the group stand and stretch. While all hands are lifted, say, "Just remember—when you're reaching up to Him as far as you can, He's reaching all the way back to you." If I'm with a women's retreat group in a very informal setting where people know one another well, I sometimes have them stand, face left, put their hands on that person's shoulders, and rub. Then ask them to face right and do the same thing. This instant back rub definitely revitalizes the crowd! Caution is in order with this technique. I would not use it in a mixed group of men and women, in a formal setting, or with a group of individuals who don't know one another.

Repeat power phrases or quotations. Slowly and distinctly make a statement that reflects one of your main points, and have the audience repeat it with you the second time. In a message on suffering I say, "'The secret of joy is *not* in having comfortable circumstances.' Say that with me." And they do. Repetition of power phrases keeps people alert and reinforces important teaching.

HOW SHOULD YOU HANDLE TOUGH SITUATIONS?

It's likely at some points in your speaking career that some tough situations will arise. The main thing to keep in mind is to remain calm and unruffled (at least on the surface). Don't let the situation disrupt what you have planned to do.

If someone asks a hostile question, diffuse the tension by restating it in a neutral way. A top speaker who had several best-selling books available for purchase at a meeting was asked publicly, "Where does the money for all of those books go?"

He responded, "The question is, 'Where do the royalties go?'" This enabled the speaker to neutralize the skeptic's question and tell about his favorite charities.

When a person is disruptive in the audience, make eye contact with the individual and, if possible, point humor his way. Say something like, "Now Jerry Smith has never made any mistakes with his children, but the rest of us need some helpful guidelines on parenting." Your eye contact shows you're not intimidated by him, and your warmth and humor disarm him.

If a baby cries or a small child makes too much noise, look at the parent and stop speaking for a moment. The audience isn't listening to you while the baby is crying anyway. Say to the parent, "How old is he? That sound makes me miss my kids. We may be able to carry on, but if your child isn't all that excited about listening to my speech, he might be happier in the nursery, which is right down the hall to your right."

If a disturbing interference occurs, such as flickering lights, a siren, or a loud sound, immediately acknowledge it and then proceed. When the distraction takes place, the audience instinctively directs attention toward it; you might come up with a clever comment that fits your theme, but in any event, say *something* about the interference. The attention will immediately come back to you.

When you are speaking in a building where other activities are taking place, have the lectern placed on the opposite side from the entrance. This will keep your group from being distracted unnecessarily if people are walking in the halls. Also, have the audience seated so that they cannot see out windows where people walking outside could capture their attention.

HOW CAN YOU BE A "CUT ABOVE" THE AVERAGE SPEAKER?

Arrive at least thirty minutes early. It relieves the chairperson to know the speaker is on time, and it gives you an opportunity to mingle with the crowd and gain rapport before you actually speak.

Never begin with an apology such as the following:

- "I had trouble finding the church, and that's why I'm late."
- "I've never been good at speaking, but if you'll bear with me . . ."
- "I've been sick all week, and almost couldn't come . . ."
- "You will probably disagree with what I'm going to say . . ."
- "It's so hot in this room, we may begin to suffocate, but . . ."
- "I have such a scratchy voice because of my cold, so I know you'll have trouble hearing me."

- "This has been such a busy week that I haven't really had time to prepare."

Refer to the messages other speakers have given and try to "tie in" to the general theme and music ministry.

Avoid naming denominations or labeling cults when you are speaking outside your own church or denominational conference.

Submit to the way the retreat or banquet is organized. Don't try to give a group advice about how things could run more smoothly unless they ask for your input.

Affirm the other speakers personally and publicly if you are sharing a platform. Let them know you're praying for them and consider the conference or retreat a "team" effort.

Make plans to stay with the group that invited you instead of disappearing to go shopping or pursuing a personal agenda. Be available for prayer times with the staff and for meals with your host.

Develop the topic you were asked to speak on instead of cleverly disguising your "prepared" messages.

Be available for counseling after you speak, but know when you should suggest that someone needs to see a professional Christian counselor.

Ask for evaluations when possible. At first this may seem risky, but ask God to help you honestly evaluate and prune each presentation so it can be the best for His glory. Realize there will always be some people who don't care for your style or topic, but that's okay. God will use someone else to reach them.

Know your time limit and finish promptly.

WHAT DOES IT TAKE TO PURSUE GOD'S EXCELLENCE?

1. Pray for God's guidance in the choice of topic, the place of ministry, and your motive for speaking.
2. Confess all known sin.

3. Be an example of the believers in your home, your business, and your social life.
4. Study the Bible consistently. Read God's instructions and requirements for spiritual leaders and teachers.
5. Realize that you are simply a vehicle for God's message.
6. Prepare your messages early. Interruptions often come at the last minute, and God is honored when we plan ahead instead of expecting Him to "come through" for us because we procrastinated.
7. Depend on God's power, not your own wit, education, or natural ability.

In a chapter like this one I have a recurring fear that you will be caught up in technique and forget that the most important part of the delivery of any message is the power of God flowing through you to the listener. Do your homework, practice your message, but above all *pray*! It is always my prayer that God will translate the message to meet the need of every individual in the audience. "The effective, fervent prayer of a righteous man avails much" (James 5:16).

S. Truett Cathy has said:

I believe God wants us to be successful . . . and yet success is not always obvious. The Chinese bamboo tree does absolutely nothing—or so it seems—for the first four years. Then suddenly, sometime during the fifth year, it shoots up ninety feet in sixty days. Would you say that bamboo tree grew in six weeks, or five years? I think our lives are akin to the Chinese bamboo tree. Sometimes we put forth effort, put forth effort, and put forth effort . . . and nothing seems to happen. But if you do the right things long enough, you'll receive the rewards of your efforts.[4]

PART FOUR

What Do I Speak About?

NINE

Getting Started

Making Introductions, Leading a Meeting, and Guiding a Discussion

In order to be a leader a man must have followers. And to have followers, a man must have their confidence. Hence the supreme quality for a leader is unquestionable integrity. Without it, no real success is possible. . . . If a man's associates find him guilty of phoniness, if they find that he lacks forthright integrity, he will fail. His teachings and actions must square with each other. The first great need, therefore, is integrity and high purpose.[1]

— DWIGHT EISENHOWER

"Carol, how did you break into speaking?" It was the same question I had heard on numerous occasions. The seminar participant obviously wanted to hear a practical, workable plan for beginning a conference and retreat ministry.

I smiled, paused, and gave my usual reply: "Very s-l-o-w-l-y." There's enough theatrical flair in me that it might be enjoyable to concoct a fail-safe formula for those of you who are beginning speakers. The ingredients would involve careful preparation of your inner spirit and your material. The obvious next step would be for your phone to start ringing, and the opportunities for sharing your message with others would multiply with every passing day.

Not so! Outstanding public speakers are not born overnight.

Usually a speaker spends a period of years in preparation before receiving widespread recognition. It's just that when the recognition comes, the speaker seems to have *instant visibility*. One of God's great blessings in the life of the beginning speaker is the *time* it takes to get started. Welcome this period of your life as a good friend, and realize that this training ground is God's way of preparing you for what is ahead.

ACCEPT LEADERSHIP RESPONSIBILITIES

List the organizations and church-related events and classes that need your skills. Most of the time these groups are looking for people who care about their goals and are willing to help out in leadership roles. You may be asked to be the emcee for a banquet, to chair a committee, or to teach a class. Say yes and use those opportunities to give needed assistance and direction to groups of people who need your services.

The benefits you receive are multiple. In addition to developing your speaking and organizational skills, you gain experience in dealing with different personality types. Use this training time to the fullest. Make it a goal to prepare as well as you would if you knew you were being paid a fee for your services.

During my high school years, my father was in his first pastorate. Our small church didn't have a large enough budget to hire a youth minister, so if any activities were held, a member of the congregation had to do the planning. Since I was not allowed to date non-Christians, I was strongly motivated to get personally involved in organizing social gatherings of teenagers. When no qualified adult was on hand to give the devotional message at the conclusion of an event, the job fell to me. At that time I never recognized the invaluable training I was obtaining for the future.

VALUE YOUR UNIQUE BACKGROUND

It was the fall of 1969, and the Vietnam War was in high gear. Most of the recent male college graduates could expect to be called into active duty soon. Since a good friend worked in the draft office, we knew Gene, my husband, would be in the next group to go for training.

We had been married only a couple of months. The prospect of the armed forces as a "next step" in our lives was not a happy thought, but it did give us a sense of direction. How well I remember turning on the news one day and hearing about the new lottery system for choosing men to serve in active duty. During the very first month of this innovative plan of selective service, Gene's birth date was one of the last drawn.

Our emotions ranged from euphoria to disappointment. We were so grateful that in God's sovereignty Gene would not have to go to Vietnam, but we were filled with unrest at the thought of having to make plans for the immediate future. No longer were our lives on hold until Uncle Sam let go. As recent university graduates, we had important, life-changing decisions to make.

We moved to a larger city where Gene could take some seminary-level Bible classes. I was trained to be a teacher, but since no positions were open at the time of our move, I sought the help of an employment agency. My "saleable skill" was typing, and I soon accepted a position as executive secretary in the marketing department of a large corporation.

A few months earlier I had obtained my degree in speech education, but I ended up typing someone else's correspondence and answering a phone. With every fiber of my being I wanted to be teaching—doing the job I was trained for: educating young people. Did God know what He was doing? Did God know that Gene wouldn't be going to Vietnam? Did God plan for my best gifts to be wasted on a desk job with limited advancement potential when I could be an excellent teacher?

Some of you are in a period of creative restlessness right now. There's an urgency within, and you know that God is beginning to give you a desire to communicate for His glory. But you're on hold. You have a job that is needed for livelihood, and you can't afford to go into speaking with no other form of income at your disposal. Some of you feel ready to speak, but no one has asked for your services. Jack Herbert once said, "To be ready to make a speech and not be asked to speak is even worse than being asked to speak when you are not ready."[2] What should you do?

As you pray for guidance, keep working hard at the job God has given you to do. I fervently believe that when you are in a right relationship with God and experience an acute desire to use your gifts for Him, He is already at work preparing you for "active duty." He also knows the field of service that will benefit most from your unique qualifications.

That year, while working in my position with the Steelcase Corporation in Grand Rapids, Michigan, I was trained by the assistant to the president of the company. I learned how to set up the format of a well-written business letter. She taught me how to compose letters that were concise and attractive—correspondence that made a statement of excellence for the reputation of the company. I was exposed to extraordinary office efficiency and outstanding management teams.

Everything I learned during my six months in a job I didn't want (and to be honest, a job I thought I was overqualified for) has now been used to make my correspondence as a speaker better and my administration of the Speak Up with Confidence seminars more effective. God was not wasting my ability on menial tasks; He was giving me the finest on-the-job training for everything I'm doing today.

INTRODUCE OTHER SPEAKERS EFFECTIVELY

A wonderful way to practice effective communication is to accept the responsibility of introducing other speakers. I wish I had kept a journal of some of the unusual ways people have introduced me at their meetings.

One weekend at an out-of-state retreat I was seated on the platform with the retreat committee in front of a large audience. The crowd was enthusiastic, and the music, announcements, and book reviews were done efficiently. It was time for me to speak, and the chairwoman walked to the lectern to introduce me. She began, "It's so good to have you here. Many in this audience have driven a great distance to be part of the special day. I know we were all hoping that Jill Briscoe could be our fall retreat speaker, but since she couldn't be here, I know we're all thankful for the speaker the Lord *did* send. I'd like to introduce Carol Kent . . ."

My initial reaction was a spontaneous desire to laugh. I had never before been introduced as the second choice, and the chairwoman's innocence and sincerity in trying so hard to present a proper introduction added to the humor. It was obvious that she didn't realize her remarks were inappropriate. Several women in the audience were visibly gasping at her comment and were looking for my reaction.

At a moment like that it would have been fun to begin my talk with a humorous reference to the introduction, but I would have embarrassed the chairwoman. The best course of action was to avoid obvious awareness of the *faux pas* and get on with my message.

What makes an outstanding introduction? What information do you need? I like the way *The Basic Meeting Manual* defines a good introduction:

> If you are introducing a speaker at a gathering of any kind, your role will be to pave the way for your speaker by building respect, creating good will, and arousing interest in the subject to be discussed. Your message to the audience should be that you are presenting a speaker whom they will greatly enjoy. Then, briefly, tell them why.[3]

To do your homework properly, request the speaker's résumé ahead of time so that you can become familiar with the individual's background and educational qualifications, but don't read from this sheet when you do the introduction.

At one meeting the emcee went to the microphone to introduce me and stated, "Before Carol Kent comes to speak to you today, I'd like to read the list of credentials and accomplishments she gave me to share with you." That moment was embarrassing for me since it appeared that I had asked the chairman to announce my qualifications, when in reality I had only sent the usual information sheet in some early correspondence with the group.

To introduce a speaker effectively, follow these guidelines:

Be enthusiastic. Your introduction should gain the attention of the audience and set a mood of anticipation for what the speaker is about to say.

Be brief. Some introductions are almost as long as the speaker's presentation. Occasionally, I am asked to give a message that someone heard on one of my CDs. If the person doing the introduction has heard the recording, there is a strong temptation to summarize my whole talk while introducing me, thus taking away from the impact of my message.

Be personal. It's fine to mention a few educational credentials or accomplishments, but try to focus on some piece of information that makes the speaker human. Mention a humorous incident, a key interest, or something about the speaker's family that is in good taste and would create a warm atmosphere. Avoid any information that could be embarrassing to the speaker.

Be appropriate. The tone used in your introduction should establish the mood for the occasion. When an audience is gathered to hear current statistics about an issue of urgent importance, too much humor in the introduction would be inappropriate.

Be accurate. One time I was introduced as the leader of an organization that I had worked for several years before. The person doing the introduction had an outdated résumé and never checked to see if it was current. Also, carefully go over the pronunciation of the speaker's name to be sure you can say it properly. The name can be mentioned in the first part of the introduction, but it should *always* be used in your concluding statement. If possible, announce the speaker's message title at this time, too.

Be prepared. Have your notes ready ahead of time. Three-by-five-inch cards work well for this purpose. Be familiar enough with your opening remarks to have direct eye contact with the audience. When you finish the introduction, turn toward the speaker, smile, and with a welcoming gesture, say, "Please help me welcome _____!" Lead the group in applause as the speaker comes to the microphone.

Ask these questions when preparing an introduction: Whom am I introducing? Where is the speaker from? What are this individual's credentials? What is the topic? Why should the audience be interested in listening? How can I create a warm atmosphere for this speaker?

Introducing other speakers can be tremendously rewarding and can provide invaluable training. In addition to the actual public speaking experience, you have the benefit of listening to gifted communicators who will provide you with new knowledge and techniques.

LEAD MEETINGS CONFIDENTLY

Most of us have sat on a committee or endured a congregational meeting where the leader had no sense of direction, and we wondered how long the aimless discussion would continue before someone moved for an adjournment. It takes very little extra time to prepare for leading a meeting in a way that will instill confidence in your leadership and create a productive climate for the group.

To lead a meeting effectively, remember these important principles:

Know your purpose. Groups meet and committees are formed because they share common goals. Try to state the main purpose of the group you are leading. Why did the group band together originally? What is their mission statement?

Narrow your aim. As you think about the meeting you are about to lead, work to narrow your aim. Write down the main purpose of the meeting. If your purpose is not specific enough to identify, you should consider eliminating the meeting because you have nothing to accomplish. Realize that some groups meet only for the purpose of connecting, which can be a worthy goal in itself, but it's still important to know your purpose.

Have an agenda. Developing an agenda will give you as the leader a sense of direction. The following general format works well for keeping a business meeting on target. Fill in the appropriate information, including the date of the meeting, names of individuals who will be giving reports, people who are in the program, and so on.

Date:
Call to Order:
Welcome and Opening Prayer:
Pledge of Allegiance: (When appropriate — some groups are
    much less formal than others.)
Secretary's Report:
Treasurer's Report:
Old Business:
New Business:
Committee Reports:
Miscellaneous Items:
Adjournment of Business Meeting:
Introduction of Program:
Closing Remarks and/or Prayer:

If you lead many business meetings, you would benefit from a more in-depth understanding of parliamentary procedure. *Robert's Rules of Order* is an excellent resource for this purpose.

Stay on schedule. There is never a more popular leader than the one who knows his or her purpose, sticks to a prepared agenda, and starts and ends the meeting on time. If you are in charge of a church function, a luncheon, or any kind of meeting that involves people presenting a program to an audience, have copies of the schedule made for everyone on the program, complete with a suggested time for each person's involvement. This creates an instant *responsibility factor* for the person who tends to take more than the time allotted.

Learn to delegate. Before going into full-time speaking, I was the chairperson of a Christian women's group. One of the most difficult functions I learned was to let go of responsibilities that someone else could handle. If you are a strong natural leader, you probably have a hidden fear that if you don't do everything yourself, it might not be done with the quality you require. By delegating tasks, you can develop leadership in others and free yourself for other areas of ministry. An organized leader who learns this lesson early will soon discover that it takes minimal time to be an effective chairperson of a group.

GUIDE A DISCUSSION GROUP

While you are waiting for invitations to speak, take advantage of opportunities to guide a discussion group. Numerous community and church-related Bible study groups need discussion leaders. You receive excellent training for future ministry as you respond to the needs and questions of individuals in a small group setting. These people often become close friends and ardent prayer supporters as God opens doors for you to minister in other places.

The structure of your group will depend on the purpose for getting together. The following guidelines are helpful for a Bible study discussion group:

Establish a warm atmosphere. At the first meeting have people split up into pairs. Each person's assignment is to get enough information from the other person to be able to introduce that individual to the rest of the group. This activity often cements a caring relationship between the two people who interview each other, and it also produces the warmth of humor when someone needs help with the pronunciation of an unusual name. Give the group about five minutes for the interview before you begin the introductions.

Prevent problems. Go over your discussion group guidelines at the first meeting in a very routine way. When people know the rules ahead of time, it saves awkwardness and confrontation at a later date.

Avoid controversial issues. Let the members of the group know that they will not be discussing doctrinal issues that divide the church. Instead, they will concentrate on the many positives in the Word of God that Christians agree on. This guideline will allow you to "keep the peace" when people of different denominations are represented in the group.

If you come to a controversial verse in Scripture, sometimes it's wise to say, "Here's a verse many responsible Christians disagree on. Rather than take the time to debate the issue today, let's just read the verse aloud. Later you can talk to your pastor about the meaning."

Encourage group participation. To guard against one well-prepared participant monopolizing the discussion, enforce a guideline that no one share again until two or three others have given responses. This will allow the shy person to make a comment without constantly being cut off by the stronger personalities in the group.

As the leader, don't give your own answers—no matter how much you enjoyed doing the study. Allow the group the opportunity of responding to your questions. Ask questions that encourage discussion: "What does that verse mean to you personally?" "What does the Bible say in this passage about . . . ?" Try to avoid questions that call for a yes or a no answer. After all, it is a *discussion* group. The only time the leader needs to volunteer answers is when no one in the class has come up with the Bible-based answer.

Use tact. When someone gives a wrong answer, instead of bluntly rejecting the response, ask, "Does anyone else have a different opinion about this question?" You're sure to have a theologian in the group who would love to give the correct answer.

If there are new Christians in the group, be careful about asking people to pray aloud. Some may never come back because of the fear of having to pray in public when they don't know how.

Emphasize careful preparation. Let participants know that the goal is to come prepared to discuss what the Bible says about the topic, not to have an inspirational "sharing session."

Pray for your group. At the first meeting, pass out three-by-five-inch cards, and ask the participants to put their names, e-mail addresses, and phone numbers on the cards. Let them know that as their discussion leader, you are committed to praying for them on a daily basis, and you would appreciate having specific prayer requests written on the cards, too. Give the group your e-mail address and encourage them to send you updates on their prayer concerns.

During the week, use the cards to pray specifically for each person. If God nudges you to call or e-mail someone and give a word of encouragement, the information is already on the card. It takes very little extra time to take an interest in the individuals in the group. For me, lifetime friendships have come out of this experience, and the quality of ministry is unsurpassed.

Honor the established schedule. Start on time, and end on time. Many people have work responsibilities and babysitters. Respect them enough to be committed to the announced timeframe of the group.

No amount of retreat and conference speaking will ever take the place of the intimacy you can know as a discussion group leader. While you are waiting for doors to open to greater speaking opportunities, enjoy the moment. The relationships you develop will be something to cherish for a lifetime.

GETTING STARTED AS A CHRISTIAN SPEAKER

In addition to the main points in this chapter, I'd like to offer some other helpful suggestions.

1. Develop a promotional one-sheet (an 8½ x 11, single-sided page that will help meeting planners to get a quick summary of what they can expect from you as a speaker). Also save an

electronic copy of this sheet that can be e-mailed to people inquiring about your ministry. This information sheet could include any of the following: (a) education, work, and ministry experiences; (b) suggested speaking topics; (c) endorsements from people who have heard you speak; (d) family information; (e) hobbies or interests; (f) books and/or articles you've written; (g) awards you have received; and (h) your name, address, phone number, website, and e-mail address.

2. Have a publicity picture taken. Be sure to choose a pose that makes you look confident and happy. Many photographers take attractive serious or reflective shots, but those pictures do not project the professional image of a dynamic speaker. The picture can be used on your promotional piece. Eventually, it will be used for newspaper publicity and retreat and/or conference brochures. Be sure to get an electronic copy of the picture with permission from the photographer to e-mail to meeting planners.

3. Join a group or take a class that will give you an opportunity to perfect your communication skills. Some possibilities are Toastmasters, Dale Carnegie courses, community college speech classes, CLASS seminars, and, of course, Speak Up with Confidence (Original and Advanced Seminars).[4]

4. Take advantage of every opportunity to speak for church and community programs. Most excellent public speakers started out by speaking for no fee anywhere they were asked. As their abilities improved, they were recommended by word of mouth, and every time they did an excellent presentation, additional requests for their services came in.

5. Become a student of other speakers, and become an expert on your subject.

This chapter has been full of ideas about what to do while waiting for the phone to ring. However, God Himself is the One who raises up leaders and opens opportunities for ministry. In my experience of working with potential speakers, I find repeatedly that God gives the desire for public ministry to the Christian whom He has gifted for this task. His timing may be different from what you anticipate, but if your desire is of Him, don't lose heart when you don't see instant ministry opportunities.

During my junior and senior years as a student in a Christian university, I was given many opportunities to speak to large groups on campus. Part of that time I taught a Sunday school class of several hundred women. After graduation, I married, moved to a new city, and sometime later combined school teaching with helping my husband in his role as a youth pastor. For four years, even though I was teaching speech, I was never invited to speak for the women of my church, and no one asked me to use my gift in Christian service.

During this time, I attended a women's retreat and realized God was convicting me of the need to get into study of the Word—to get prepared for speaking for His glory. (You'll read that story in a later chapter.)

Sensing a desire to work with women and to teach the Bible, I prayed, "Lord, if this desire is of You, please bring an opportunity. If this is of me, for my own human ego, please take away the desire, and do not open the door for me to speak." That week I received a call inviting me to speak for a mother-and-daughter banquet. The first year I spoke for two banquets. The next year there were more invitations, and someone asked if I would prepare a retreat workshop. I accepted. Then came a home Bible study. Finally, someone asked if I could present three messages for a retreat weekend.

I honestly don't remember when I began turning down more invitations than I could possibly accept. I had no clever marketing technique. I didn't even have an attractive publicity picture or a professional brochure in those early days. God opened the door for an opportunity to serve. I worked hard to prepare the best talk I could give. Someone in the audience told others . . . and they told others . . . and they told others . . . and that's how my ministry multiplied. "Present yourselves to God as being alive from the dead, and your members as instruments of righteousness to God" (Romans 6:13).

TEN

Your Life Story Has Potential!

Preparing Your Personal Testimony

Each generation of the church in each setting has the responsibility of communicating the gospel in understandable terms, considering the language and thought-forms of that setting.[1]
— FRANCIS SCHAEFFER

My life was completely ruined! As a child, I had been the victim of both physical and mental abuse. By the time I became a teenager, my life had gotten progressively worse. Alcohol and drugs were my only escape from an unbearable home situation.

On two occasions, I tried to commit suicide. Guilt was my constant companion. There are no words to properly express my disappointment upon awakening in a hospital room and finding I was still alive.

Rather than learning from my past mistakes, I continued to make unwise choices. Quitting school at age sixteen meant I needed to find a job — and I still had a drug habit to support.

Good jobs were hard to find, so I married the first man who showed any interest in me. Two months into the marriage he came home drunk, and later that night I was back in the hospital with two broken ribs and a fractured jaw. I had married a man exactly like my father!

A PERSONAL OBSERVATION

No, the opening paragraphs of this chapter are *not* a description of my life story. I have painted this exaggerated word picture not to be funny or to make light of someone else's hardships, but to demonstrate a major fallacy among many would-be speakers.

Somewhere along the line we have picked up the distorted notion that unless we have a gutter-to-glory story, we really have no testimony to tell. There are exceptions, of course—professional athletes, beauty queens, or individuals who have overcome mental or physical disabilities. These people seem to have profound illustrations and dynamic deliveries. Add to that list professional Christian musicians who skillfully weave their personal testimonies throughout inspirational concerts. By comparison, your life may seem rather uninteresting and your talent nonexistent.

My main point is this: Don't miss the indescribable joy of sharing your experience of finding faith in Christ because you think it lacks the drama, intrigue, and intensity of the outstanding personalities you have heard speak. Many of these well-known people have been mightily used of God to share the redeeming power of Christ with a world in need.

But your life story has potential, too, and God can use what might seem ordinary to you to prepare a heart to receive the gospel message.

A BEGINNING PLACE

In working with concerned Christians who would like to grow in their ability to communicate effectively, I have discovered the personal testimony to be an excellent beginning place. I think there are three major reasons for this.

1. Jesus commanded us to go and make disciples. Matthew 28:19 makes it clear that one of our main purposes as believers is to

win others to Christ. Sharing your discovery of the Lord Jesus Christ is an excellent way to introduce them to Him.

2. Your life is unique. No one has ever had your experience; no one has come to know the Lord precisely the way you have. Your story is interesting because it's vastly different from that of anyone who has ever lived before.

3. There is a great need for speakers. Many Christian organizations and churches sponsor evangelistic outreaches, and there is an ongoing demand for qualified people to speak at these events.

I'm not suggesting that all Christians should be speakers. It would be very difficult to speak if everyone was on the platform and no one was in the audience. God gives different gifts to individuals. However, many people who have sensed God's leading to prepare and have received invitations to speak have turned down these opportunities repeatedly.

Sometimes fear is the culprit, but more often it's a simple matter of not knowing how to prepare. For many, the last speech you remember giving was an oral book report in an English class twenty or thirty years ago! The memory of a bad experience at that time could be holding you back now.

I chuckled recently when I read Mark Twain's advice to a friend who was not excited about making a speech. He said, "Just remember —they don't expect much!" Twain's advice is humorous, but if you're like me, there are other considerations. If you're going to go through the work and stress of preparation, why not do a good job? As Christians, we have the most important message of all, and it deserves to be told with dignity.

THE FIRST WORKSHOP

Some time ago I was coming to the end of a major commitment as teacher of a women's Bible study. Before I left for the final meeting with the discussion leaders and staff, I opened the Bible and read,

Forget the former things;
do not dwell on the past.
See, I am doing a new thing!
Now it springs up; do you not perceive it?
(Isaiah 43:18-19, niv)

Not one to take Scripture out of context, I simply meditated on those verses during the next few weeks. Slowly, God brought many things to mind. Over the years of teaching Bible study, working in my church, and being involved in Christian organizations, I had met many people who had the desire to be better communicators of God's truth, but they didn't know where to begin. There were letters on my desk from women in several states and Canada, saying they knew I was a former speech teacher, and they wondered if I could offer them any tips on getting started as a speaker. Then came phone calls from men and women in my hometown asking if I could help them put their personal testimony into a meaningful talk.

It had never occurred to me that the Lord wanted me to use my training and background not only to speak, but to equip others to do the same. After much prayer, I started a small local Christian Speakers' Workshop in my living room. We began going over the how-tos of putting together a Christian testimony. It soon became apparent that it would help to have a classroom atmosphere with access to a data projector, so we moved our meetings to a church.

The participants made tremendous progress as they prepared and presented their weekly assignments. An invaluable aid to learning was the class's feedback after each speech; eventually, printed evaluation forms were used for that purpose. People were affirmed immediately in what they did well, and they appreciated finding out where they could improve.

The results from that first group have been encouraging. Some of the most shy participants faithfully did their homework and are now speaking with wonderful results and much less fear.

One woman called after sharing her testimony at a luncheon for the first time. "Carol," she said breathlessly, "there were five people who accepted Christ after my talk today. I can't believe that God could use my ordinary story to draw someone to Christ. I feel so privileged!"

A few of the participants realized that public speaking was not something they felt led to pursue. However, all of them agreed that learning basic speech skills had helped them organize their thoughts and communicate what they wanted to say to others. People who organize their ideas and present their convictions in an understandable manner feel more confident and have far greater effectiveness.

A NECESSARY REMINDER

Redemption of a lost soul is God's work—not something that a human being manipulates through having a clever vehicle and an attractive, well-packaged speech. I've been rereading the biography of John and Betty Stam, missionaries who were martyred for the cause of Christ in 1934 at the hands of Communist soldiers in China.

Their story is an uncomfortable irritant, causing me to ask questions I'd rather not face. Am I spending my time on the *urgent* or the *important*? Am I giving my life's energy to something that ultimately counts? Is my faith worth dying for?

I became acutely aware that John and Betty Stam did not attain *that* level of faith in God overnight. It was a lifestyle, a commitment, and an unshakable conviction years before it was put to the ultimate test.

While Betty was a student in college, she wrote a letter to one of her younger brothers. The essence of this letter embodies my major premise in this chapter:

Nobody can force a single soul . . . to Christ. All that the followers of Jesus have to do, all they can do, is to lift up

Christ before the world, bring Him into dingy corners and dark places of the earth where He is unknown, introduce Him to strangers, talk about Him to everybody, and live so closely with Him and in Him that others may see that there really is such a Person as Jesus, because some human being proves it by being like Him. That is positively all the Lord asks us to do for Him, because He Himself does all the rest.[2]

Yes, God draws people to Himself (see Ephesians 1:11), but we human beings have the responsibilities to live exemplary lives and faithfully proclaim the good news. It was Hudson Taylor who said, "I used to ask God to help me. Then I asked if I might help Him. I ended up asking Him to do His work through me."

A WISE PLAN

Praise God for grandpas! They make time to dig for worms and take kids fishing. They answer hard questions and help children work on big projects that require counsel and skill.

Our son, J.P., was born in a hurry. Once his legs were strong enough, he was off and running—and he hasn't slowed down yet. When J.P. was quite small, Grandpa Afman took him for a leisurely ride on a sunny afternoon, and halfway through the drive, he suddenly announced, "Grandpa, you're wasting my time!"

He didn't mean to be disrespectful, but there were other things he wanted to do that *seemed* more important. J.P. has always had enough creative ideas, energy, and enthusiasm for any ten children. The problem is that he sometimes begins a project *before* it is carefully planned.

Not long ago my husband and I had to go out of town to a convention, and we asked Grandma and Grandpa to care for Jason. We returned home to find J.P. and Grandpa hard at work, drafting careful plans for a tree house. They had documented the exact measurements for every piece of wood that would be used in the project. I was rather impressed that our son had taken the time to draw the plans before slapping the house together, and I complimented him on the organization and planning.

"Grandpa showed me something, Mom." He picked up the Bible on the kitchen desk and turned to Proverbs 15:22. He read, "Without counsel, plans go awry." He went on, "It's true! I'm going to have a better tree house because Grandpa's helping me make plans first!"

What a valuable lesson! Whether it's a tree house or a personal testimony, careful preparation ahead of time will be extremely beneficial to you and your audience.

A PRACTICAL APPROACH

In putting together a testimony, some people work *chronologically*, telling their life story from birth to the present, citing important events and decisions along the way. Others use a *crisis point* approach, developing the theme of the talk around one main event, such as a major illness or an emotional trauma. A number of people prepare *Christian growth* presentations, first explaining their decision to trust Christ and then pointing out steps to a more mature walk with the Lord, using personal illustrations.

Several Christian organizations and evangelism programs have customized other worthwhile frameworks for organizing and presenting a testimony. The plan I'm giving you in this chapter is not the only way to prepare your story — it's *one* possibility among many. Since there is an overwhelming need for speakers at evangelistic outreach luncheons and banquets, the format described next will have the aim of reaching the nonbeliever with the gospel.

Study the flow chart "Your Personal Testimony" on page 179, concentrating for a moment on the Scripture verse: "This means that anyone who belongs to Christ has become a new person. The old life is gone; a new life has begun!" (2 Corinthians 5:17, NLT).

Most speakers who are invited to present after-dinner evangelistic talks are given about thirty minutes to speak. How can anyone tell a life story in a half hour? It's an impossible task. That's why it's essential to choose the most important material and structure it carefully. Think in terms of "universal needs," "common bonds," or "felt needs" as we discussed in an earlier chapter. There are specific attitudes and emotions common to most of us. Words like *fear*, *love*, *stress*, and *joy* immediately recall memories from the past.

Think of your life. What attitude or emotion would best describe your life *before* coming to know Christ? If you had an early childhood conversion, think of your time of spiritual immaturity. Now think of the opposite, positive attitude or emotion that describes your life since becoming a Christian or since experiencing spiritual growth. Read through the following examples; perhaps you'll find a comparison that reflects your own experience.

NEGATIVE	POSITIVE
(Before Christ or as an immature believer)	(After Christ or as a growing Christian)
aimlessness	direction
fear	trust
anger	love
low self-esteem	healthy self-worth
despair	hope
ego-centered	Christ-centered
emptiness	fulfillment
stress	peace
sorrow	joy

The possibilities for additional comparisons are endless. By building the framework of your testimony around specific attitudes or emotions common to the audience, a very personal application will be made by each listener. I could tell an illustration about my life and interest or amuse an audience, but if I identify the felt needs of the

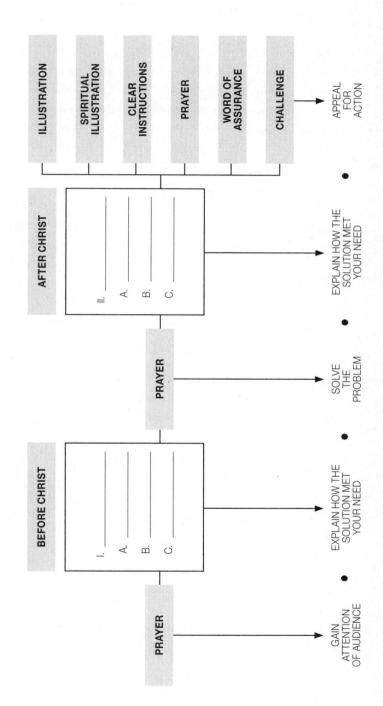

YOUR PERSONAL TESTIMONY

"Therefore, if anyone is in Christ, he is a new creation;
the old has gone, the new has come!" —2 Corinthians 5:17 (NIV)

PRAYER

BEFORE CHRIST

I.
A.
B.
C.

PRAYER

AFTER CHRIST

II.
A.
B.
C.

ILLUSTRATION

SPIRITUAL ILLUSTRATION

CLEAR INSTRUCTIONS

PRAYER

WORD OF ASSURANCE

CHALLENGE

GAIN ATTENTION OF AUDIENCE

EXPLAIN HOW THE SOLUTION MET YOUR NEED

SOLVE THE PROBLEM

EXPLAIN HOW THE SOLUTION MET YOUR NEED

APPEAL FOR ACTION

group, someone out there is thinking: *She's telling my story. Something like that happened to me. I know just what she's talking about!*

Read through the following "Personal Testimony Worksheet." I'll explain the structure in greater depth on the next few pages. After you've had a chance to study this material, come go back to the worksheet on page 179 and fill in the blanks with ideas about how you could structure your life story.

We've done the preliminary homework. Now let's go step by step through the process. As each section is discussed, you will see a suggested time frame for each portion of a thirty-minute presentation. If you have a longer speaking time, you can make adjustments.

1. Rapport (about five minutes)

Turn back to chapter 5 and try to find an attention step that would interest your audience in your message. For an evangelistic talk, keep the opening very light. Your main tasks in this segment of the speech are to *build a bridge* of warmth between you and the audience and to *introduce your theme.*

According to the dictionary, a *theme* is a main subject with repeated variations. Its purpose is to give continuity to the whole. A theme will make the difference between a choppy presentation, with a series of illustrations strung together, and a smooth-flowing story, held together by a central idea. It takes some time to develop a good theme, but it's well worth the effort. It could involve a repeated word or phrase, a visual aid, a song or a series of songs, or any creative idea that would fit the story of your life.

Some tested theme ideas include the following:

A single word. The wife of a surgeon used the word *enough* as a theme throughout her talk. For a while she lived off the self-esteem of being the wife of a respected professional, but it wasn't enough. She thought she needed a new house to bring her fulfillment. The house was so grand that it took two years to build, but soon after they moved in, she discovered it wasn't enough. After a series of illustrations, all

PERSONAL TESTIMONY WORKSHEET

I. ***Rapport*** (about five minutes) Build a bridge and introduce your "theme."

II. ***Before Christ*** (about five to ten minutes) Identify an attitude or emotion that describes your life before salvation. Share two or three personal experiences that picture that attitude.

III. ***How You Came to Know Christ*** (five minutes) Give the specific steps in salvation while telling how you came to know the Lord personally. Keep it conversational, while explaining how you recognized that Jesus, the sinless Son of God, came to the earth, died on the cross, and rose again. Share how you recognized your need, accepted Christ's forgiveness, and received Him as Savior. Use Scripture to illustrate and document.

IV. ***After Christ*** (five to ten minutes) Identify the positive change in the attitude or emotion you described in section II. Share two or three personal experiences that show the wonderful difference that Christ has made in your life.

V. ***Conclusion*** (five minutes)

A. Tell a concise illustration.

B. Include a spiritual application at the end of that illustration.

C. Give clear instructions. Example: "In just a moment I'm going to pray. In that prayer I will give you an opportunity to pray a prayer like I did many years ago, when I invited Jesus Christ into my life. If this is something you desire to do today, please pray silently with me, while I pray aloud."

D. Pray. Be sure to mention the following:
   1. Address God the Father.
   2. Acknowledge God's Son, Jesus Christ.
   3. Thank Him for His death on the cross.
   4. Admit sin and the need for forgiveness.
   5. Ask Christ to come into "my" life and to take over the controls.
   6. Thank Him for His gift of eternal life.
   7. Pray in Jesus' name.

E. Give a word of assurance. Example: "If you prayed with me just now, welcome to the family of God!" Encourage them to share their decision with you or with the person who brought them.

F. Leave with a challenge.
   1. A meaningful quotation.
   2. A concluding thought.

establishing her search for meaning, she came to the climax of the presentation with an account of coming to know Christ personally. She said, "For the first time in my life, I discovered that He is *enough!*"

Musical terms. If you are a musician, take musical terms, such as *time signature*, *rests*, and *holds*, and share illustrations and applications of the times when God put you on hold and so on.

Series of songs. Diana Pintar shares the idea of telling her story through a series of well-known song titles. She starts out with thoughts best expressed by "Is That All There Is?" When she found an answer to her emptiness in the decision to trust Christ, she says that she heard the song that has become a reminder of her commitment: "I Have Decided to Follow Jesus." She skillfully explains the joys and challenges of her decision and ends her testimony with "Something Beautiful."

A love story. My sister Jennie Afman Dimkoff uses this theme and begins by saying, "How many of you really enjoy a good old-fashioned love story? Have you ever read the last page of a compelling romance before you read the rest of the book?" Jennie tells our mother's exciting story of getting seven proposals during the days of World War II and her decision to marry our handsome father. She goes on to relate her own search for love and her choice to receive Jesus as Savior, after understanding the greatest love story of all. She emphasizes the importance of reading God's love letter to us — the Bible. Jennie ends by stating, "We all want love stories to have happy endings, but today you have the opportunity to write the ending yourself in response to God's love letter to you."

A book. Have you ever thought of your life as a book? Ginger Sisson has created a creative theme for her story around the chapters of her life. The title of her book is *I Am a Rare Gem*, since that's what her father called her as a child. She believed it and went on to write her chapters. After each of her ego-centered chapters, she tells how the titles changed when rewritten by the Chief Editor, almighty God.

Ginger's Chapters	Rewritten God's Way
1. "I Am Smart"	"You Are Wise"
2. "I Am All-Together"	"You Are Whole"
3. "I Am Tough"	"You Are Strong"

Ginger summarizes her life by saying she has been "a marshmallow in a steel shell." Her obvious application for the audience is, "What chapter are you in? Will you start now to let the One who is wiser than you begin the editing of your book?"

A visual aid. An audience will always remember your talk longer if you use the power of the visual. Since a data projector is unavailable in many luncheon or dinner locations, a hand-held visual can be more effective for a testimony presentation.

For months I prayed that God would help me find a creative vehicle for telling my very ordinary story. One of my earliest memories involves asking Jesus to come into my heart; I was five years old at the time. I'm a preacher's kid who didn't go into rebellion as a teenager or a young adult. It certainly didn't seem like much of a story to tell! (My testimony changed many years later when my only child was arrested for a heinous crime, but that's another story. You can read about it in *When I Lay My Isaac Down*, NavPress.)

As I thought about it, I realized that my "common bond" with my audience could be *low self-esteem*. As a child and as an emerging teen, I never felt pretty enough or smart enough. The positive was that God took a girl who never felt that she measured up and changed the inferior perception into *confidence in Him*! There was my comparison outline. Next I needed a theme.

I went back to my knees and prayed for an inspired idea to give my story continuity. At the time, I was teaching drama, speech, and English and did a lot of supplemental reading. One day I ran across a booklet by Dr. Sidney Simon called *The IALAC Story*. The story was about a boy who wore an invisible sign around his neck that said IALAC. The letters stood for "I Am Lovable and Capable," and pieces of the sign would be torn off when he had conflicts with his parents, peers, teachers, and even himself. Every time he lost a portion of his self-esteem, another part of the sign was ripped off.

Dr. Simon is a secular educator. His suggestion for the boy with self-esteem problems involved teaching him to pick himself up by his bootstraps by choosing different reactions to all of those negatives. At the end of the story, the author encouraged the reader to tell a personal version of the IALAC story.

Something clicked as I finished reading. *There* was my idea—only the solution to the problem would be quite different from the one in the booklet. We don't pick ourselves up; God puts us back together. The Greek meaning of the word *peace* means "bringing all the fragments into oneness." That's what God did in my life. He put me back together in completeness and wholeness. The homework began, and soon my own version of *The IALAC Story* was born, complete with the IALAC sign I wore around my neck as a visual aid.

2. Before Christ (about five to ten minutes)

By this time you've determined your comparison outline; you've decided on a theme; and you've prepared an attention step (rapport) around that theme. Now it's time to work with the negative word you chose that describes your life before coming to know Christ. If you made a childhood decision, this section refers to your time of immaturity as a Christian. Develop two or three illustrations from your life that depict the negative emotion or attitude you described.

In my presentation, I tell the "Big Lips" story here, since it is a clear illustration of my sense of low self-worth. I have a visible IALAC sign around my neck, and as the boy seated behind me says, "She *does* have big lips, doesn't she?" I rip off a huge piece of the sign. The main purpose of this portion of the message is to *establish a need for change.* It is impossible to lead someone to Christ who doesn't acknowledge being a sinner.

3. How? (five minutes)

This is a vital portion of your story because you are *solving the problem* by explaining how you came to know Christ. Take the time to explain the specific steps in salvation while telling your own experience. Make it one person's discovery of Jesus Christ.

Avoid getting too technical or using theological jargon that might confuse or intimidate an unbeliever. Delete references to a specific denomination if you are speaking outside of your own.

You have one goal—to explain how you recognized that Jesus, the sinless Son of God, came to this earth, died on the cross, and rose again. (Don't forget to include the Resurrection. You're asking people to commit themselves to a *living* Savior.) Tell how you recognized your need, accepted Christ's forgiveness, and received Him as Savior. Use Scripture to illustrate and document.

Once when I was very young, I was listening to a radio program called "Unshackled," the voice of the Pacific Garden Mission in Chicago. The program dramatizes stories of people who have had significant life changes. I don't remember what the story was about that day, but I do remember my heavy conviction. Turning to my mother, I said, "Oh, Mama, I'm such a sinner! Do you think that Jesus would come into my heart?"

Mother got the Bible, turned to Romans 3:23, and read, "For all have sinned, and come short of the glory of God" (KJV). She turned to another verse and continued, "For the wages of sin is death; but the gift of God is eternal life through Jesus Christ our Lord" (Romans 6:23, KJV). She then reminded me of what I had heard from my earliest days in Sunday school—Jesus, the sinless Son of God, came to this earth as a babe in a Bethlehem manger; He grew up in that insignificant town of Nazareth; at age thirty, He went into His public ministry, and even the religious leaders of the day did not believe that He was the promised Messiah. Finally, that same Jesus was hung on a cross, bearing in His body my sin and the sin of the world; He rose again and is preparing a place in heaven for those who believe. That day I eagerly got on my knees with Mother at my side and invited the Lord Jesus to be my Savior and Lord. It has been the most important decision of my life!

If you made a very early decision to trust Christ, you might want to use the flashback technique, as I did in this section. I was called "Big Lips" a few years after my conversion, but since my goal is to reach non-Christians in this talk, I want the audience to get to know me and feel comfortable without feeling as if I'm "preaching at" them. Because I use the words "When I was very young . . ." at the beginning of the "How?" section, they realize I'm going back to an illustration from my early childhood.

4. After Christ (five to ten minutes)

Now it's time to *explain how the solution met your need.* Identify the positive change in the attitude or emotion you described earlier. For me, it was "confidence in Christ." I am a person of worth and dignity in His eyes and can leave an inferior self-image behind. He created me for a purpose, and I'm a member of the family of God. It's beneficial to illustrate this point with two or three personal experiences that show the difference Christ has made in your life.

5. Conclusion (five minutes)

You're almost finished, and it's time to *appeal for action.* This is the weakest portion of many evangelistic talks. Sometimes a listener wants to begin a personal relationship with Christ but doesn't know how to experience it because the speaker's conclusion was too vague. Do your homework carefully.

Tell an illustration. Years ago I heard the story of a missionary who was serving the Lord in Korea. A young Korean woman was expecting a baby, and on Christmas Eve she went into labor. There was a major storm in progress, but the woman knew if she could just get to the home of the missionary, she would have the help she so desperately needed to bring her baby into the world. She put on her winter wraps and started out alone, on foot. She was several miles from home when her labor pains grew in frequency and intensity, and she knew she could not make it to her destination.

She got beneath an old bridge that afforded a bit of shelter. There, alone, in the middle of the night, she gave birth to a beautiful baby boy. She immediately removed her coat and then, piece by piece, the rest of her clothing. Carefully, she wound every item around her baby until he looked like a cumbersome little cocoon. Then she fell asleep, too exhausted to do anything else.

The next morning brightly dawned, and the missionary awoke with a song in her heart. It was Christmas Day, and there were so many people she wanted to see. She packed the car and started on her way. A few miles down the road the engine sputtered, and the car finally stopped on top of an old bridge. As the missionary opened the door to go for help, she thought she heard a baby crying. Following the sound, she went under the bridge where she found a tiny baby boy — very hungry, but very much alive. Next to the infant lay his mother — frozen.

The missionary picked up the baby and took him to her home. In time, she was permitted to adopt the boy. As the years passed, she told him how his biological mother had given her life that he might live. Her son never tired of hearing the story, and he asked her to repeat it again and again.

On his twelfth birthday he asked the missionary to take him to the burial place of his mother. When they arrived, there was snow on the ground, and he asked his missionary mother to wait while he went to the graveside alone. She watched her son as he trudged through the snow, tears streaming down his cheeks. In amazement, she saw him slowly unbutton his coat, remove it, and gently lay it on the snowy grave. Next, he removed his shirt, trousers, shoes, and socks and carefully placed each item on the grave of the mother who had given her all for him.

The missionary could take it no longer and went to her son, placing her coat around his bare, shivering shoulders. Through his tears, she heard him as he asked, "Were you colder than this for me, Mother?" And he knew that she was.

Include a spiritual application at the end of the illustration. Here's one example: "That's a beautiful picture of what the Lord Jesus Christ did for you and me. The Bible explains that He left heaven's glory to come to this earth. He came in complete obedience to His Father's will to give His life that you and I might experience forgiveness of sin and eternal life by trusting Him as Savior and Lord."

Give clear instructions. I like to respect the intelligence of my audience by announcing ahead of time that I will give them an opportunity to pray with me. Since I give a careful explanation of *what* I'm going to pray, the non-Christian has a chance to consider whether or not to make a decision for Christ at that time.

Lead in prayer. You could say, "In just a moment I'm going to pray. In that prayer I will give you an opportunity to pray a prayer like I did many years ago when I invited Jesus Christ into my life. If you would like to know beyond any doubt that you have been born into the family of God, as we pray, tell God that you know you're a sinner, that you know Jesus died for you on the cross of Calvary, and that He rose again. Then I'll give you a chance to invite Him to take over the controls of your life. If this is something you desire to do today, please pray silently with me while I pray aloud."

Include the following in your prayer: (1) address God the Father; (2) acknowledge God's Son, Jesus Christ; (3) thank Him for His death on the cross; (4) admit sin and the need for forgiveness; (5) ask Christ to come into "my" life and to take over the controls; (6) thank Him for His gift of eternal life; and (7) pray in Jesus' name.

Give a word of assurance. You could say, "If you prayed with me just now, welcome to the family of God!" Encourage them to share their decision with you or with the person who brought them. If possible, place a booklet in their hands that will clearly explain the decision they have just made. Always ask the leader of the group you are addressing if a booklet is to be distributed. If one is not available, request permission to use your own, making sure that the material you use is not controversial. (My favorite booklets to use for this purpose are "Would You Believe It?" published by Stonecroft Ministries, Kansas City, Missouri; "Four Spiritual Laws," published by Campus Crusade for Christ, Orlando, Florida; and "Steps to Peace with God," published by the Billy Graham Evangelistic Association, Minneapolis, Minnesota.)

Leave with a challenge. Conclude your talk in a positive way. There will always be people in the audience who have chosen not to respond to your invitation. What do you want them to leave with? Often, a meaningful quotation or a concluding thought is all that is necessary. I close my testimony presentation with my theme: "I'd like for all of you to know you are very lovable and capable. Will you say that with me?" In unison, everyone in the audience enthusiastically repeats: "I am lovable and capable!" Then I finish by saying, "And you are, not just because I think so, but because God *says so!*"

A CONCLUDING CHALLENGE

Many of you are ready to go to work on preparing your story. Ask yourself these questions upon completing your homework, and be willing to do heavy editing if necessary.

- Is the gospel message clear?
- Have I glamorized sin by taking up too much time to explain the details of my life "before Christ"?
- Is the rapport step something that would interest a non-Christian in wanting to hear more?
- Do I have a clear theme that gives continuity to the whole message?
- Have I "stretched the truth" by exaggerating to make a good story better?
- Would any of my family members be embarrassed because of my choice of illustrations?

- Is my story too long?
- Have I used words that a pre-Christian can understand?
- Have I asked someone to honestly critique my message?
- Will I trust God for the results?

Years ago Blaise Pascal said, "There is a God-shaped vacuum in every heart." More recently, A. Wetherell Johnson, the founder of Bible Study Fellowship, said,

> Man searches for his own fulfillment in life in many ways, but where is lasting fulfillment to be found? A career comes to an end; attaining to a great position of wealth or power fails to satisfy one's deepest longings. Surely there must be something more to life! Has life on earth any meaning if death is its final end? Many people experience a sense of frustration by life's seeming emptiness and brevity. . . . What I would have missed had I not cried out as an agnostic to God and discovered that I was "created for commitment" to Him and to His purpose for my life.[3]

For some of you, the concepts in this chapter are new and difficult to understand. You may have the recurring question in the back of your mind, *Have I ever experienced this for myself?* Don't wait. Investigate the claims of Christ, and discover the truth for yourself!

ELEVEN

The Most Exciting Book of All!

Teaching the Bible with Clarity

*The Christian who is not diligently involved in a serious study
of Scripture is simply inadequate as a disciple of Christ. To
be an adequate Christian and competent in the things of God
one must do more than attend "sharing sessions" and "bless me
parties." We cannot learn competency by osmosis. The biblically
illiterate Christian is not only inadequate but unequipped.*[1]

—R. C. Sproul

Caught! There I sat at 10:30 a.m. in front of the television, munching
on potato chips. I had already sat through *The Today Show* and a
popular talk show; now I was deeply engrossed in one of the new game
shows.

Suddenly, the door burst open and in walked my husband—unexpectedly. He had forgotten some insurance forms he needed at the
office, and *there* I was! It was too late to run, and there was no place to
hide. After one quick look, he burst into uproarious laughter. "If only
your audiences could see you now—just a woman of leisure!"

I knew he was only kidding, but it didn't seem very funny to me.
The thought *had* occurred to me earlier that I should be doing something important—reading my Bible, preparing a message, or writing a
book—but it was much easier to vegetate in front of the TV and eat.

I ran to the bathroom and looked in the mirror. The reflection star-
ing back at me brought only one word to mind—*slothful!* My hair was

matted on one side; both eyelids were puffy from too much water retention (I'd eaten potato chips the day before, too); and my stunning garb
consisted of a housecoat that should have been thrown out two years
ago complemented by worn-out beach sandals and a baggy sweater,
worn over the housecoat because I was cold.

I worked up the nerve to smile at my reflection and sarcastically
announced, "What a *dynamic* Christian leader! What a *model* of virtue
and discipline!"

Later that day I tried to shake the image of the earlier hour. Sitting
at my desk, I couldn't resist the impulse to look up the words *sloth* and
slothful. According to Mr. Webster, a slothful person is characterized by
a "disinclination to work or exert oneself." That description is followed
by three words — *indolence, laziness*, and *slowness*. I had seen a sloth
once. It's a slow-moving South American mammal that does nothing
but eat and lounge around in trees.

As I closed the dictionary, my conviction was heavy. Picking up
my Bible, I turned to its concordance and looked up the same words.
Here's what I discovered:

The way of the slothful man is as an hedge of thorns. (Proverbs
15:19, KJV)

Thou wicked and slothful servant. (Matthew 25:26, KJV)

That ye be not slothful, but followers of them who through
faith and patience inherit the promises. (Hebrews 6:12, KJV)

Not slothful in business; fervent in spirit; serving the Lord.
(Romans 12:11, KJV)

There is no doubt about it. Slothfulness, by God's standards, is *not*
a desirable trait! I slipped to my knees and confessed my sin.

Many of us have been slothful about having regular and consistent

Bible study. This "disinclination to work or exert oneself" in becoming literate in Scripture is all too common. Many of our churches are crying for competent teachers who are capable of handling the Word of God with accuracy and authority.

Most of us *want* to know the Word better, but the desire is not compelling enough to cause us to give up something else to make the time.

Last summer our family enjoyed a wonderful week on the sandy shores of beautiful Lake Michigan at Maranatha Bible Conference in Muskegon, Michigan. I was presenting the Speak Up seminar during the afternoons, and every morning we sat under the teaching of Dr. Earl Radmacher, former president of Western Seminary. In one of his messages, Dr. Radmacher said, "The average man in America has not been able to whip the demands of the materialistic society in order to give himself to concentrated, intensive study of the Word of God and yet, he wants to be a leader. Leader of what? . . . With what?"[2] Even though statistically there are more women involved in organized Bible studies than men, this continues to be a stingingly relevant question for women as well as for men. Dr. Radmacher continued,

> William Culbertson, then president of Moody Bible Institute, said, "The average student coming to Moody today with the advantage of a high school education knows less of the Word of God than a man thirty years ago with a third grade education." We are growing progressively illiterate in the Word of God.[3]

Most of us who had the advantage of growing up in the church can talk "Christianese" well enough to get by. And it isn't that we don't spend *any* time in the Bible. Every day we pray for a flash of divine guidance and then go "luckydipping."

Dr. R. C. Sproul defines this technique in his book *Knowing Scripture*:

Luckydipping refers to the method of Bible study in which a person prays for divine guidance and then lets the Bible fall open to wherever it happens to open. Then, with eyes shut the person "dips" his finger to the page and gets his answer from God wherever the finger lands on the page. . . . This is not a sound way to use the Bible. I don't think . . . the Holy Ghost had this in mind when the words were penned.[4]

CONFESSIONS OF A SLOTH

These words are being written by a recovering luckydipper. I did have spurts of guilt about my lack of attention to the Bible, and I was greatly encouraged and challenged by people who taught the Word well. Yet for a while, nothing changed in my self-defeating study behavior. Even slothful people do enough to stay comfortable. I studied the Bible just enough to get by.

Positive change did not take place overnight, but the first major jolt occurred at a women's retreat. There were thirty-five hundred women seated in Miller Auditorium on the campus of Western Michigan University for the fall Winning Women Retreat. I had invited a close friend who was a new Christian. She had come to the Lord as a direct result of the consistent witness of her son's second-grade public school teacher.

Jeannie was overwhelmed by the whole retreat. She had never even been with two hundred believers all in one place before, and there she was with thirty-five hundred! Have you ever heard that many people sing together? It's powerful! When all stood and began lifting the rafters on "How Great Thou Art," I noticed that Jeannie wasn't singing. She was looking up, smiling broadly, her eyes glistening with tears. The group continued: "Then sings my soul, my Savior God to Thee. How great Thou art! How great Thou art!"[5] Jeannie squeezed my arm and said, "Carol, if this is earth, what must heaven be like?"

That day I looked at Christianity through the eyes of a baby believer. Her enthusiasm was totally spontaneous, and her desire to read and understand the Bible was insatiable. We laughed and cried, listened to speakers and took notes, talked and prayed.

I hesitate to tell you what happened next. My pride wants you to see me as a totally rational and not too emotional person. Seated in the auditorium, we were listening to the last speaker. During the message, I was moved in my inner being. I can't tell you the content of the message or the Scripture reference. The name of the speaker isn't relevant, either. It was God's time to get a message through to me. There were no lightning bolts, and nothing supernaturally visible took place, but the Holy Spirit was speaking to me as He often speaks to people today—with consistent, powerful, compelling conviction. God's presence and His love were engulfing me.

In the next few minutes as the meeting ended and people left the auditorium, I couldn't move. There I was—a young wife, a school teacher, a church worker, and a preacher's kid. I had a degree in speech education, and it had never entered my consciousness that there were *women* with a God-given gift to teach for His glory. I knew there were no gender differentiations in Scripture with regard to spiritual gifts (see Romans 12:4-8; 1 Corinthians 12:27-31; Ephesians 4:11-13). My students and my peers in the field of public education had confirmed my teaching gift with awards and plaudits. But what was I doing for God? Was I in any way using my best gift to serve Him? Before we left for home that day, I confessed my apathy to the Lord and committed myself to systematic study of the Word of God. I knew if He ever opened doors for me to use my gift for Him, I would need something of substance to say.

A few days ago I ran across this quote by an anonymous author: "God sometimes blesses a poor exegesis of a bad translation of a doubtful rendering of an obscure verse of a minor prophet." No wonder no one took credit for saying it! It is true, however, that God always honors His Word, and given out through the faithful lips of a willing servant with a poor delivery, it will still accomplish God's purpose. But how much better it is to prepare to the best of our God-given ability and to consistently grow in our understanding of the Word and in our ability to make it understandable to others.

COMMITMENT TO STUDY

Start where you are. Don't waste precious energy explaining, rationalizing, or apologizing for not having been a committed student of the Bible before now. The philosopher Plato was right when he said, "The beginning is the most important part of work."

For the Bible student, this means choosing to turn off the TV when it would be easier to relax and be entertained. It means establishing a *place* to study where you have a surface to write on and enough space to open reference books; it helps if your location is not in the center of activity in your home. It means commitment to a *habit* of a regular, specific time block so that you follow through with reading, researching, taking notes, and praying, even if you don't *feel* like it. It means spending some discretionary income on necessary books and online study helps instead of on personal amusement. It means considering how serious you are about studying the Bible and preparing to teach others.

I began this new era of my spiritual development by preparing to teach a neighborhood Bible study. In the next few years, God opened doors for me to become director of women's ministries at a large church in Fort Wayne, Indiana. One of my major roles was to teach a growing women's Bible study. Upon moving to Michigan a short time later, I began teaching an international Bible class for women in Sarnia, Ontario, and Port Huron, Michigan.

In the beginning of my Bible-teaching days, I would read a passage of Scripture, comment on individual verses, and add colorful illustrations that held the interest of my audience. I knew in my heart that something was missing, but I couldn't quite identify it. With a degree in speech education from a Christian university, I knew the basics of outlining, telling illustrations, and "packaging a talk," but I was never schooled in homiletics because I wasn't a Bible major.

When I accepted the invitation to teach for an international Bible study organization, the training included my "missing link." It was almost as if someone had turned on a light in a dark room. Suddenly, I brimmed with creative ideas and looked at every passage of Scripture with new eyes.

The next section of this chapter is not intended to be an exhaustive discussion of sermon preparation. Some of you will wish it were more technical—but that's okay. You will go on to seminary or to advanced training in Bible school, and that's as it should be. My aim is to help heretofore unmotivated or untrained potential Bible teachers to have a beginning place.

What I am about to teach you has transformed my life and embodies the most important information in this book. Even if you never step behind a lectern to speak, this approach to Bible study could revolutionize your personal devotions.

CONSIDER THE SOURCE

The Bible, in its original, God-breathed rendering transcribed by holy men of God, is *word for word* true. Second Timothy 3:16-17 says,

> All Scripture is given by inspiration of God, and is profitable for doctrine [That's *what* you believe], for reproof [It shows you where you're wrong], for correction [It shows you how to take what's wrong and make it right], for instruction in righteousness [*Instruction* is translated from a Greek word that means "the training of a child from infancy to maturity"], that the man of God may be complete, thoroughly equipped for every good work.

The Bible is the story of the redemption of humankind, and it has the answers for today's problems. Haddon Robinson says,

> God speaks through the Bible. It is the major tool of communication by which He addresses individuals today. . . . Through the preaching of the Scriptures, God encounters men and women to bring them to salvation (2 Timothy 3:15) and to richness and ripeness of Christian character (2 Timothy 3:1-17). Something awesome happens when God confronts an individual through preaching and seizes him by the soul.[6]

Although the author's comments are addressed primarily to men studying for the ministry, there is profound truth for all of us who teach the Bible. We have an accurate, authoritative, powerful source for speaking material, the living Word of God. We need to study it consistently and instruct others accurately.

CLARIFY THE STEPS

1. Read the passage or chapter you are going to teach in at least two different translations. Sometimes a careful reading of the Scripture in a translation you haven't read for a while will trigger some creative ideas regarding the passage. For our purposes in this chapter, let's read John 5:1-15:

> [1] After this there was a feast of the Jews, and Jesus went up to Jerusalem.
> [2] Now there is in Jerusalem by the Sheep Gate a pool, which is called in Hebrew, Bethesda, having five porches.
> [3] In these lay a great multitude of sick people, blind, lame, paralyzed, waiting for the moving of the water.
> [4] For an angel went down at a certain time into the pool and stirred up the water; then whoever stepped in first, after

the stirring of the water, was made well of whatever disease he had.

⁵ Now a certain man was there who had an infirmity thirty-eight years.

⁶ When Jesus saw him lying there, and knew that he already had been in that condition a long time, He said to him, "Do you want to be made well?"

⁷ The sick man answered Him, "Sir, I have no man to put me into the pool when the water is stirred up; but while I am coming, another steps down before me."

⁸ Jesus said to him, "Rise, take up your bed and walk."

⁹ And immediately the man was made well, took up his bed, and walked. And that day was the Sabbath.

¹⁰ The Jews therefore said to him who was cured, "It is the Sabbath; it is not lawful for you to carry your bed."

¹¹ He answered them, "He who made me well said to me, 'Take up your bed and walk.'"

¹² Then they asked him, "Who is the Man who said to you, 'Take up your bed and walk'?"

¹³ But the one who was healed did not know who it was, for Jesus had withdrawn, a multitude being in that place.

¹⁴ Afterward Jesus found him in the temple, and said to him, "See, you have been made well. Sin no more, lest a worse thing come upon you."

¹⁵ The man departed and told the Jews that it was Jesus who had made him well.

2. Use a legal pad or a notebook, and number to fifteen on the left-hand side of the paper. That's how many verses we're going to use for our message.

Next to each number, write a phrase that summarizes what each verse is about. It doesn't have to be a complete sentence or carefully structured wording. All you're doing is answering the question, What does the Bible *say* in each of these fifteen verses?

If you are in the mood for a challenge, don't read the example that follows until you've had a chance to do this exercise for yourself. See what you come up with based on your reading of the verses. Be careful not to write what you think they mean. We'll get to that later.

Verse-by-verse summary of John 5:1-15:

> verse 1: Jesus went to Jerusalem after feast
> verse 2: pool of Bethesda there
> verse 3: disabled and sick wait for water to move
> verse 4: angel stirred water—first one in healed
> verse 5: man there—invalid for 38 years
> verse 6: Jesus' question—"Do you want to get well?"
> verse 7: man replies—no one to help
> verse 8: Jesus heals him
> verse 9: man well—it's the Sabbath
> verse 10: Jews upset about mat-carrying on Sabbath
> verse 11: man says healer told him to
> verse 12: Jews ask, "Who?"
> verse 13: man doesn't know
> verse 14: Jesus tells man to stop sinning
> verse 15: man said Jesus made him well

Stop for a minute, and think about how you normally prepare to teach a Bible lesson. Unless you are the exception, this is often what happens. You know a week ahead of time that you have a teaching responsibility for Sunday morning. You intend to spend a little time working on it every night. But Monday night, football is on TV—the Dallas Cowboys—your favorite! Tuesday night you have a church board meeting and get home too late to study. Wednesday night is prayer meeting. Thursday night you notice that the grass is getting long, and you decide to mow it to avoid being a bad testimony to the neighbors. After that, you're too tired to study. On Friday your sister and brother-in-law arrive with their three kids to spend the night. Both families drive to the state park on Saturday for a leisurely day at the lake.

By Saturday night, you're worn out, irritable, sunburned, and not feeling much like teaching tomorrow morning, but it's too late to back out. Grabbing the lesson plan, you see that the Scripture to be taught is John 5:1-15. Bonanza! You know that story so well you don't even have to reread the passage before you throw your teaching notes together. On Sunday morning you muff your way through a sharing session, hoping for lots of discussion that will camouflage your lack of preparation.

Does this hit home? The details of this scenario change depending on your work schedule, gender, and level of activity in any given week, but the result is often predictable. The summarizing of every verse is time consuming, but when you finish, you have *experienced* the passage. You have picked up on small details you might have otherwise overlooked. But the most important aspect is this: You have the opportunity for God to speak to you through this Scripture before you are responsible for teaching others.

Look at the "Bible Teaching Guide" on page 202. You have already done the verse-by-verse description. Now it's time for the next step.

3. Find three to five main themes (number can vary) in these verses. Using the sheet you've just completed, mark a line between the end of one thought or idea and the beginning of a new one. All the while, pray for insight on the best way to teach this lesson. When you decide on the divisions, make additional notes. They might look something like this:

1. verses 1-4 — Disabled people wait
2. verses 5-9 — Man sick for thirty-eight years is healed
3. verses 10-13 — Complaints from crowd
4. verses 14-15 — Jesus tells man to sin no more

Note that you haven't come up with a cleverly worded outline yet. You haven't had to worry about sentence structure, either. You

BIBLE TEACHING GUIDE

"My son, if you accept my words and store up my commands within you, turning your ear to wisdom and applying your heart to understanding, and if you look for it as for silver and search for it as for hidden treasure, then you will understand the fear of the Lord and find the knowledge of God." —Proverbs 2:1-5 (NIV)

VERSE BY VERSE DESCRIPTION

vs. 1 _____
vs. 2 _____
vs. 3 _____
vs. 4 _____
vs. 5 _____
vs. 6 _____
vs. 7 _____
vs. 8 _____
vs. 9 _____
vs. 10 _____
vs. 11 _____
vs. 12 _____
vs. 13 _____
vs. 14 _____
vs. 15 _____

THREE OR FOUR MAIN IDEAS

1 Handicapped people wait

2 Man sick for 38 years is healed

3 Complaints from crowd

4 Jesus tells man to sin no more

SUBJECT SENTENCE

SPECIFIC AIM

FINAL OUTLINE

I. Disabled people (1-4)
   A. _____
   B. _____

II. Discouraged invalid (5-9)
   A. _____
   B. _____

III. Demanding crowd (10-13)
   A. _____
   B. _____

IV. Delivered man (14-15)
   A. _____
   B. _____

ADD ILLUSTRATIONS AND APPLICATIONS

I. _____
   A. _____
   B. _____

II. _____
   A. _____
   B. _____

III. _____
   A. _____
   B. _____

IV. _____
   A. _____
   B. _____

DECIDE ON RAPPORT

WORK ON CONCLUSION

AIM: to cause audience to see areas where they are spiritually disabled and choose to get up and walk

APPLICATION QUESTIONS:

1. What's your spiritual infirmity and how long have you had it?
2. Are you longing for the moving of His Spirit in your life?

are simply deciding what verses will be grouped together when you *do* prepare the final outline. There are many different possible divisions, which make for tremendous variety even when two people speak on the same passage.

4. The next step is to prepare a *subject sentence*. Reread your descriptions of the verse groupings, and try to write a sentence of ten words or less that embodies the essence of the entire passage. For example, Jesus heals man physically and spiritually, but the Jews complain.

Why is this a necessary step? It's apparent that this sentence is not a catchy title for a message, nor is it a sentence you would use in the manuscript of your message. So why go to the effort of coming up with one sentence that summarizes the whole fifteen verses?

Most of us make even general conversation too wordy. We take ten minutes to tell what should take three minutes, and still we aren't sure what "nugget of truth" we are trying to get across. Charles Spurgeon once said, "If you ask me how you may shorten your sermons, I should say, study them better. Spend more time in the study that you may need less in the pulpit. We are generally longest when we have the least to say." When I haven't prepared a subject sentence for a Bible study message and I'm asked what my talk will be about, my answer is too long. I don't even know the essence of the passage, so how can I expect my audience to understand it?

5. Since your next step is to write out your *aim*, you need to do some additional work. You'll be deciding what you want your audience to *do* as a result of hearing this message.

Before deciding on my aim, I like to do some research. I know what the passage says, but what does it *mean* in the light of the people who lived in Jerusalem at that time? Is there a word used in a certain verb tense that gives a clue to the meaning of the text? Is there some history that I should check regarding the Sheep Gate that was by the pool? Since the Bible is word for word important, nothing in the passage is trivial.

Some of you are *digital* thinkers. You see most things in black and white. You are practical, not too emotional; efficient; and capable of following directions accurately. The rest of you fall into the category of *pictorial* thinkers. You see the dramatic elements in everything. When you dream, it's in living color. Your descriptions make things better than the original. As you read, you're not looking at words on a page, you're viewing a motion picture with moving figures and colorful surroundings. You *smell* the flowers and *hear* the surf. You *experience* the book you are reading. Digital thinkers get upset with you because you tend to exaggerate, and they think you should be more practical. You don't mind because you *know* you enjoy life more than they do!

For a moment I'd like for all of you to become pictorial thinkers. Let's journey through John 5:1-15, and imagine what it would have been like to be there. We're in Jerusalem by a pool called Bethesda. Can you *see* the blue water? There are five porches connected to this area by the pool, and there's a sheep gate nearby. In his commentary on the gospel of John, Arthur Pink says, "This is the gate through which the sacrificial animals were brought to the temple—the 'lamb' predominating, hence its name. The sheep gate, then, points us at once to Christ, and tells of His cross."[7]

All over the porches and next to the water are sick people—blind people, lame people, paralyzed people. Can you *see* the mats? Can you *smell* the air, remembering the last time you were in a convalescent center with lots of sick people? Besides that, sheep walk through this area; they're cute to look at, but they *smell* terrible.

The people were all there with one hope—to be healed by being the first one into the pool when the water was stirred. I wonder if some of them were on the edge of the pool, waiting to leap in at the right moment. Others might have had relatives nearby ready to dump them over the edge. The rich could have hired help for the occasion—anything to be first!

Jesus enters this scene and begins moving around the Bethesda compound. In spite of the smell, He moves from person to person, *touching them and looking at them with eyes of compassion.*

When Jesus comes to one man, a man who has had an infirmity for thirty-eight years, He says, "Do you want to be made well?"

By my standards, that seems to be a dumb question. The man might have sarcastically responded, "Are you kidding? Do you think I've enjoyed being sick for thirty-eight years?" But everything I know about Jesus must influence my understanding of this passage. Jesus *never* asks dumb questions.

Aha! Why then would Jesus have asked the question? What possible reasons could the man have for *not* wanting to get well? He might have had to get a job. People would quit waiting on him. He might have been experiencing fear of the unknown or fear of change. Being sick for thirty-eight years wasn't great, but he was used to it. Living outside his "comfort zone" would be risky, new, frightening. Perhaps Jesus wanted him to see the utter helplessness of his condition.

The man's answer amazes me. Instead of saying yes, he tells Jesus he has no one to put him into the pool at the right time. Somebody always beats him into the water.

There are two things we don't know about this part of the passage. The vocal inflection would tell us a lot. Did he have a whiny tone and say, "I don't have anybody to help me"? Second, where was his mat located? Was he next to the edge of the water, or was he halfway up through the crowd of people, a safe distance away from possible healing and the responsibilities that would follow? We don't know how long the poolside healings had been going on, but don't you think the fellow could have figured out how to "beat the system" after thirty-eight years?

Jesus heals him, and he is *immediately* well. Oops! Jesus heals him on the wrong day! It's the Sabbath, and the Jews are spitting mad.

At this point I have to ask myself, *Did Jesus know what day it was? Did He make a mistake? Did He forget Jewish law in the busyness of His day?* Of course not. He wanted to heal the man on a day that would cause the Jews to consider the errors of their overly legalistic traditions.

When the Jews tell the man it isn't lawful to be healed on the Sabbath, the man's response gives us another clue to his personality profile. The first time we hear him speak, he blames others for his problem. ("There's nobody to help me.") Now he passes the buck again. ("Don't look at *me*. I can't help that I got well. The man who made me well told me to walk. It's not my fault.") The man has been sick for thirty-eight years and doesn't even get the name of the person who heals him.

For those of you who think I'm being hard on this fellow and reading into the Scripture what isn't there, look at verse 14. When Jesus sees the man in the temple, He says, "Sin no more." The *New American Standard Bible* records it as, "Do not sin anymore." The *New International Version* is translated, "Stop sinning." We don't know the exact nature of the sin, but it might have been a severe attitude problem.

All right. Be honest. Would some of you digital thinkers admit that you enjoyed your pictorial walk through this passage? While you're trying to see the passage in light of the culture of the times, use lots of reference books. Check a Bible atlas to visualize geographically where the scene took place. Read the notes on the passage in a good commentary. Make a list of key words or recurring words, and look them up in an expository dictionary of New and Old Testament words.

For instance, the word *infirmity* as used in this text means "a missing connection between your brain and your body." Doesn't that make your mind run wild? Have you ever had a missing connection between your brain and your body? Think of the numerous applications . . . but we're getting ahead of ourselves. Application questions will come later.

Right now you need an aim. You've digested the passage. You've found out what it means—culturally, historically, geographically, and grammatically. While you are studying, pray that you will choose the aim that will best meet the needs of the group you are ministering to. What are some possibilities for this passage? You could state the aim in these ways: (1) to cause my audience to get rid of bad attitudes; (2) to practice true Christianity instead of religious ritualism; (3) to identify areas in which they are spiritually disabled and choose to get up and walk; or (4) to accept Christ's healing power.

I'm sure you could think of several more possible aims for this same Scripture. After you determine your aim, all the preparation you do for the specifics of the message will revolve around having the audience understand and respond to that aim.

Are you getting excited about what this method of Bible study could do for you? For your students?

6. It's time to prepare the final outline. Look back at your three or four main ideas in light of your aim and the study you've done. What kind of structure would work best for this passage—alliterative, comparison, questions, key word, acrostic?

Take a look at these examples, but realize that the possibilities of creative outlines at this point are numerous.

Alliterative Outline for an Adult Audience:

- Disabled People (verses 1-4)
- Discouraged Invalid (verses 5-9)
- Demanding Crowd (verses 10-13)
- Delivered Man (verses 14-15)[8]

Creative Outline for Christian Medical Community:

- The Outdoor Clinic
- Miraculous Healing
- Malpractice Suit Filed
- Arbitration

Creative Outline for Youth:

- Hanging Out at the Pool
- Lifeguard Arrives
- Pool Inspectors Come
- Life Saved

(Application: Stop fooling around or you'll drown!)

Think about who is in your audience. Then pray that God will fill you with His creativity as you put an outline together that will minister specifically to that group.

7. When you have decided on your outline, you are ready to add subheadings under each point with appropriate illustrations and application questions. You need to answer the question, *What does it mean to me?* Are there any personal illustrations you could use that would fit this message? You can use definitions, anecdotes, quotations, and Bible examples along with your personal illustrations.

An example of how to develop a subpoint appears next. (Keep in mind that this outline is more detailed because it will be used for your speaking notes.)

I. Disabled people (verses 1-4)
   A. People different
      1. Impotent (Do you feel without power in your spiritual life?)
      2. Blind (Has it been too long since your eyes were opened to a new spiritual truth from the Bible?)
      3. Halt (Are you limping badly, with an up-and-down experience with the Lord?)
      4. Paralyzed (Do you feel withered up spiritually?)
   B. People alike
      1. All waiting for the moving of the water
      2. All longing for the intervention of a miracle
   C. Application questions
      1. What's your spiritual disability, and how long have you had it?
      2. Are you longing for the moving of His Spirit in your life?[9]

Think of one or two applications for each main point that will help the audience apply the message to their own lives. I like to ask these questions after each section of the outline, but some speakers prefer to make all their applications at the end of the message. This is up to you.

8. The heavy work is done. All you need are the finishing touches. Decide on a rapport step that fits the theme. If my aim in the message was to cause my audience to get rid of bad attitudes, I might begin with the Grand Canyon story you read in chapter 1. It tells about my own bad attitude and creates warmth with the audience so I can quickly get into the "meat" of the message.

The last of the preparation is the conclusion. You can use an illustration that capsules your aim, or you can use a series of application questions. For example: "Do you have an attitude problem that needs to go? What is your spiritual disability? As Jesus said, 'Do you *want* to get well?' Are you ready to quit blaming others for lack of spiritual success in your life? Jesus said it's time to stop sinning! Will you choose to get up and walk today?"

Close with prayer or a call for commitment, being sensitive to the audience, the location, and the needs of the particular group of people. Trust God for the results. When you have faithfully prepared and have given out the Word of God, *something* will happen. It might not be visible to you at that moment, but God's Spirit speaks through His Word. You can count on it every time the Bible is the source of your speaking material. This study and preparation method will work with almost any biblical passage. I challenge you to put it into practice and see what a difference it will make in your life and ministry.

CHALLENGE TO SPEAKERS

Caught! Suddenly, without warning, you and I will come to the end of this life, and we will stand before the King of kings. There will be no time to run and hide, no time to put our lives in order, no time to begin doing the important work of studying His Word and teaching others, no time to make up for lost opportunities. Time, as we know it, will have run out—gone forever.

As you stand before your Maker, what will He see? A slothful person? Oh, yes, born again, but characterized by a disinclination to work at the important things—indolent and lazy! Or will He say, "Well done, thou good and faithful servant!"? The choice is up to you.

PART FIVE

How Do I Get Organized?

Organization — Inside and Out

Preparing for Leadership and Organizing Your Material

Most people don't think in terms of minutes. They waste all
their minutes. Nor do they think in terms of their whole life.
They operate in the mid-range of hours or days. So they start
over again every week, and spend another chunk unrelated
to their lifetime goals. They are doing a random walk
through life, moving without getting anywhere.[1]

—ALAN LAKEIN

The emcee was exceptionally funny. I was seated in the audience at a large convention, and the opening ceremonies established a circus theme, complete with clowns, helium balloons, popcorn, and a live elephant. The great jungle animal thundered down the center aisle, causing quite a stir on the main floor. Immediately behind him were men in uniform carrying fancy silver-plated shovels.

The master of ceremonies adjusted his glasses and calmly stated, "An elephant eats five hundred pounds of food a day and retains only 5 percent of that amount." The crowd was roaring with laughter. I didn't hear the next part of the presentation because that simple statement had set my mind in motion.

Over my lifetime I have taken in volumes of information from a variety of sources—gifted teachers, inspirational speakers, the media, classic literary works, and a variety of other books. Add to that the bene-fit of being raised in an extraordinary Christian home with consistent exposure to Bible teaching and godly principles for living. Missionaries from around the globe were frequent guests in our home, giving me a wonderful background of cultures, religions, and people from faraway places. What have I done with such a wealth of information? Have I retained even 5 percent of that valuable input? The main problem for most of us is that we live each day as it comes with no thought for the future; we don't realize the benefit of developing a system for retaining information and remembering meaningful experiences. Much of the richness of past knowledge and experience is lost or, at best, blurred.

This fact can be disheartening to people who go into public speaking. A few years ago you never dreamed you would be preparing outlines and delivering talks. You may be a lot like the old man who was seen in the park last week. The lettering on his T-shirt said, "If I'd known I was going to live this long, I would have taken better care of myself." Likewise, if you had known you would be speaking or teaching at this stage of your life, you would have prepared by getting training and filing resource material for future use. Don't fret about the past. Read on — it's not too late to begin organizing your life and resources.

PREPARE FOR CHANGE

Do you remember when you were a new Christian? If you are like most people, some aspects of your life went through a major overhaul. I dearly love the way C. S. Lewis retells an illustration he borrowed from George MacDonald:

> Imagine yourself as a living house. God comes in to rebuild that house. At first perhaps, you can understand what He is doing. He is getting the drains right and stopping the leaks in the roof and so on: you knew that those jobs needed doing and so you are not surprised. But presently He starts knocking the house about in a way that hurts abominably and does not seem to make sense. What on earth is He up to? The explanation is that

He is building quite a different house from the one you thought of—throwing out a new wing here, putting on an extra floor there, running up towers, making courtyards. You thought you were going to be made into a decent little cottage: but He is building a palace. He intends to come and live in it Himself.[2]

The Christian life is a dynamic process, and growth sometimes means being stretched beyond your comfort zone. For some of you, the *stretching* process has included public speaking—something you thought you'd never do. I believe God delights in watching us allow His strength to be made perfect in our weakness. As you continue to prepare for God's next step in your life, stay on the growing edge and welcome new opportunities and challenges as a part of His plan for your future.

BECOME A LISTENER

Remember my class of students who defined the word *communication*? Their consensus was, "Communication is talking without a wall building up. It's hearing what was said and knowing what was meant. Sometimes it involves a look, or a touch, with no words at all. It's sharing in such a way that the other person really understands what you are saying. Listening is the hardest part of communicating."

For years the experts have been telling us that listening is the most important part of communication, but I was surprised that junior high–age young people realized that truth, too. Some of us have developed negative behaviors that we substitute for listening; "topping" and "leaving the room" are just two of them.

The technique of topping involves asking someone a question about work, ministry, or family. The person responds and then pauses for a breath of air. That's your signal. During the moment of silence, you lunge into the conversation with a lengthy description of your own fulfilling job, your Bible study group, or your unique children. The truth is that you don't want to listen at all. You want an excuse to talk about yourself.

This next nonlistening behavior—leaving the room—is normally used on family members or close coworkers. Your family and friends should know that you are intelligent enough to do more than one thing at once, and you're a busy person. While you are supposed to be listening, you are shuffling papers or working on a project without giving that person eye contact. By grunting occasionally or making a comment, you convey the message that you are listening. At times you physically move into the next room, again verbally assuring the person that you are still listening. Does this sound familiar?

The tragedy occurs when you are talking to someone who has indicated a need for counseling. You look at your watch and realize you'll be speaking again in ten minutes, so you mentally go over your outline. All the while you look at the person you are counseling and nod your head a bit in agreement and empathy. When the person bursts into tears and says, "And what should I do now?" you don't know what to say because you *mentally* left the room several minutes earlier.

As leaders, we need to practice active listening. Have you ever noticed how a small child will put both hands on your cheeks, pull your face down to his eye level, and say, "Listen to me!"?

Children are masterful at teaching us something that is true of adults, too. We all love to have our statements acknowledged by eye contact, a gentle nod, and a soft word as others listen to us. We need to wait for them to finish their sentences. We must let them know we *want* to hear what they have to say because they are important to us.

Besides establishing rapport, good listening skills are invaluable for building your resource file for speech material. As you glance back through this book, notice the number of illustrations I have included that are the direct result of people I have met or speakers I have heard.

COLLECT RESOURCE MATERIAL

What is your present system for gathering speech material? Some of you are savers. For several years you've been collecting great illustrations and quotations from bulletins and newsletters. You know a good story when you hear it—and your Bible looks like a filing cabinet. Papers are sticking out of the pages, and the binding is getting fragile from the continual flood of important stuff worth saving that is stuck inside the front cover. It's a little embarrassing when you drop your Bible, and twelve people have to help you pick up everything that fell out, but at least you've made an effort to collect valuable material.

Savers can't bear the thought of cutting articles out of periodicals, so they keep *everything*, just in case it might be needed someday. Boxes of material are hidden in closets, under beds, or in cupboards, just waiting for a day when there's time to sort through it. That day never seems to come.

Is there hope for you? Yes! Mark Twain said, "A round man cannot be expected to fit into a square hole right away. He must have time to modify his shape." Saving everything is a difficult habit to break, but with concentrated effort, you can become a *selective saver*. Try these suggestions.

Magazines

I subscribe to many different Christian magazines as well as to secular news magazines. My time is limited, so as I read, I mark anything that is potential speech material and clip it, even when the magazine is new. As ideas start flowing, I make notes in the margins about possible ways to use the information. Sometimes I write out application questions that could be used with a specific story. Why not cut up your magazines as you read them, and recycle great material into your messages while it is still current?

As your eye scans an article or website, look for key information that will help you update existing speaking material. For instance, "Teen suicide is the third leading cause of death among young adults and adolescents fifteen to twenty-four years of age."[3]

I had already prepared a talk for a fund-raising banquet for a nationally known Christian youth organization. After reading those statistics, I added them to my challenge. After quoting from the article, I said, "These figures are staggering! The fact that you are here makes a gigantic statement regarding your interest in being a part of the solution to this nation-wide problem. As you give your gifts of influence, time, and support to this organization, you are helping to make a difference in your world."

Some of my favorite periodicals for getting reusable illustrations and ideas are as follows:

- *Leadership* is an outstanding quarterly journal that devotes each issue to only one topic. What a gold mine!
- *Christianity Today* is a more scholarly magazine that will keep you up-to-date on current trends and people. Thinking Christians should read this magazine. It may be a bit academic at times, but it's good for you.
- *Discipleship Journal* is a must if you do many devotional talks. The biblical content is excellent for personal growth or for sharing with others.
- *Time* or *Newsweek* will keep you current on what's happening in the world.
- *Reader's Digest* is still one of the most valuable resources for anecdotes and real-life stories. Check your library for old issues. The jokes are just as good as those in the current issue, but less well remembered by your audience.
- *The Christian Communicator* is a valuable magazine for speakers as well as writers because organizing a talk and writing an article are similar in the developmental stages.

Subscribe to any periodical that will keep you up-to-date on the needs represented by the people who are the focus of your ministry. Other helpful magazines for specialized ministries are *Marriage Partnership*—biblical advice for couples; *Today's Christian Woman*—the needs of Christian women; and *Focus on the Family*—marriage and parenting.

The exclusion of a magazine from this list means nothing. None of us can afford to subscribe to every periodical. Find out which ones offer the best reusable material to blend with your personality and sphere of ministry.

Newspapers

Read the front page of a newspaper every day. Many of us as Christians are accused of being so heavenly minded that we are no earthly good. It speaks well of our credibility as thinking, educated human beings to refer to something that is currently happening.

USA Today is tops for giving recent statistics on a variety of current trends and topics. In a small box at the bottom of each major section you will find this information. At least twice a week this newspaper has statistics that I can use in a talk. Huge sums of money are paid to gather this data, yet you have purchased it for a few cents when it comes in your daily paper. Audiences love current statistical information and immediately think you are well informed when you include it in your messages. It adds credibility and dignity to your talks with very little extra effort on your part.

Check the comics. Some of my most amusing anecdotes come from reading the late Charles Schulz's delightful and revealing "Peanuts" comic strip. I identify with Charlie Brown—and so do millions of other people. If you speak on family relationships, refer to the "Family Circus" comics.

Newspaper advice columns carry some controversial material, but occasionally you'll find some real "keepers" in that section of the paper. Keep your eyes open, and develop an instinct for knowing reusable material when you see it.

Books

Above all, read books regularly. My personal goal is to skim at least one book per week. That may seem like an unrealistic achievement on weeks that are full of speaking engagements and numerous activities, but you will be amazed at how easily you can work it in if you use miscellaneous minutes for this purpose.

I carry a book with me to the doctor's office and the dentist's office. I read while I'm waiting in airports. If someone is meeting me for lunch and I arrive early, out comes my current reading material. The best way to find time to read is to turn off the TV after the evening news.

Whenever I'm with people who are stimulating, informed, and growing Christians, I ask them what they've been reading. Those book titles go in my notebook and help to make up my reading list. A caution is in order here. It's easy to get caught up in reading only one genre, such as self-help books, novels, science fiction, the classics, motivational books, and so on. We all have our favorite style of writing. Don't limit your growth by getting stuck in a rut. One of the most overlooked types of reading material today is the biography. I encourage you to read the life stories of the great leaders who have changed the course of history.

Keep three-by-five-inch cards or sticky notes handy while you are reading. Abbreviate the title of the book, and as you come across great quotations or illustrations, write them out or summarize them. It is important to cite page numbers, too. I am convinced that the only speakers who struggle over not being able to come up with new illustrations are not reading, or they have never developed a system for remembering the things they observe every day.

A great reminder comes from Harvey Ullman: "Anyone who stops learning is old, whether this happens at 20 or 80. Anyone who keeps on learning not only remains young, but becomes constantly more valuable regardless of physical capacity."

DEVELOP A FILING SYSTEM

The Internet, the computer, and palm-held devices have drastically changed the way we collect and store information. I store outlines, illustrations, and anecdotes electronically and in hard-copy files. I am totally convinced that for the speaker, there will *always* be a place for the filing cabinet.

There are days when my mind is empty of ideas, and I go to my trusty files and look at ideas for speeches that were placed there months or even years ago. Sometimes I will find the perfect illustration for a specific talk when I am looking randomly through my idea files. If I had only a computer on those days when my memory and creativity are not "clicking" properly, I would have no idea what file to pull up on the screen. There is also the problem of needing hard copy for everything you have stored electronically. There is simply no substitute for a well-developed filing system. In the next section I'll tell you how my files are organized. Don't try to incorporate all the ideas into your system overnight. Evaluate your present needs as a teacher or a speaker, and customize a system that will work best for you.

Before labeling file folders, you need a place to store them. The ideal place is a *filing cabinet*. If that is not financially feasible for you right now, check on the availability of *file boxes* in an office supply store. They come in a variety of colors and are made of durable cardboard that works very well for short-term storage purposes.

The first folders you label will be for reference material and can include the following:

Rapport Steps

Whenever you come across a great idea for opening a talk, clip it or write it down and put it in this folder. Sometimes I'll find a good beginning for a talk while reading a book. I write the idea down and later place it in this file, complete with the title of the book and the page number it was quoted from. If you ever write an article or a book, you'll be very glad you recorded the information and its source.

General Illustrations

There are many stories you hear or read that would not be the perfect way to begin a talk, but they have excellent potential for being used in the middle of a message. File them here.

Concluding Illustrations

Outstanding illustrations for concluding a talk do not turn up every day. They come from a variety of sources—people you talk to, books and magazine articles, and a host of other places. Be alert to the type of story that directs people to think about a specific attitude or behavior change. Some stories have an obvious salvation application. The more you listen to excellent Christian speakers, the more you will become aware of the type of illustration that directs the attention of the audience to the aim in a message.

Poems

When you find a great poem that could be used in a message, it's easy to lose track of where you read it. Even if you don't write out the entire poem, at least place a card in this file that tells its general theme, the book it's in, and the page number you found it on.

Remember that some of the greatest poems you could ever use in a talk are in your church hymnal. Before the services in your church start, read all the verses of a hymn that you haven't sung in a while. Could you use it as an illustration in one of your messages? I have rarely heard Elisabeth Elliot speak without quoting all the verses of an old hymn within the body of her message. As a child, she memorized many hymns, and she has discovered a great depth of meaning and application in those songs.

Frequently Used Illustrations

This file contains my "best of the best" stories, poems, and rapport steps. It doesn't replace the above-mentioned files, but it stores material that I've used before and feel very comfortable with. This file has gone all over the country with me because I'm never at a speaking engagement without it. I arrive to speak with my prepared messages, but occasionally something happens in a retreat or a conference that I wasn't expecting. Perhaps the atmosphere is perfect for a certain illustration that I've used before but haven't included in the message notes.

With my special file nearby, I can make last-minute changes that will enhance the quality of the program.

Electronic Presentations

Because I believe people always learn more easily by seeing an outline, I use PowerPoint when I'm teaching or speaking. In addition to my outlines, these presentations contain key Scripture verses and quotations that I am refering to during my messages.

Genesis Through Revelation Folders

What have you done with the sermon notes you've collected over a lifetime of hearing great preachers and speakers? Take the time to label sixty-six file folders with the names of the books of the Bible. When your pastor does an expository series of messages on one of the Epistles or one of the Gospels, you'll have a place to put the notes. Imagine what these files will look like after a few years. When you are asked to teach a class on a specific book of the Bible, you can go to this file and have the notes on every message you've ever heard on that book at your fingertips.

Topical Files

Many subjects do not fit under a certain book of the Bible, but you would like to collect information on topics that might make good seminar or retreat workshops. Look back at the notes you took while reading chapter 3. What topics were you interested in developing (parenting, stress, personal testimony, leadership, etc.)? Label one file folder for each topic that interests you, and save all articles, anecdotes, and quotations that will give you material for your research.

You need another set of topical files labeled for every major holiday. Great seasonal material is hard to come by, and you may prepare a message for a Christmas coffee in October before the current holiday magazines are in your hands. Many speaking engagements are planned around holidays, and it's wonderful to have anecdotes that fit the occasion. Don't forget to have folders for Father's Day and Mother's Day. Many of your first invitations to speak may be for banquets for fathers and sons or moms and daughters.

Current Study or Class Folders

If you teach Sunday school or a Bible study group, you normally know how many weeks are in the series before you actually begin teaching. Label a folder with the subject of each lesson in the series *before* you prepare the first message. Become well acquainted with your general theme for the series. As you read, collect any material that would fit a specific message, and file it in the appropriate folder ahead of time. When the time comes to prepare the current message, you will already have some possible illustrations and research done. You also have a folder already labeled, so when you finish that message, you have a place to store your notes. If you did an excellent job of teaching, you will probably be asked to repeat the series in the future.

Specific Speaking Engagements

If you are already doing quite a bit of speaking, label one folder for every engagement. You will receive letters from program planners giving you the theme of the meeting, a map to the location, and other details. It's wonderful to have everything that pertains to a speaking engagement in one place.

I have a file drawer for all future engagements organized chronologically; the first folder I see is for my next engagement, all the way through a couple of dates for conferences four years from now. When I am interrupted just before leaving for an engagement, I don't worry or panic. All the information I need for that meeting is already in the first folder in the drawer. I can grab it on my way out and feel confident that I'm not forgetting anything. When I get home, I write down what I spoke on, including the rapport step and concluding illustration I used. I also make a note about the outfit I wore. If the group ever asks me back, it will be very helpful for me to know what message I've already given.

I put this information in the folder before it goes to a different file drawer. Past engagements are filed alphabetically according to the way I will most remember the event or place. When the group calls to schedule me for another time, I pull the file and have "instant memory" of key individuals and details related to the group. People think you're wonderful for remembering so much about them, and all you've had to do is take a few minutes to keep good records.

CUSTOMIZE A NOTEBOOK OR AN ELECTRONIC DEVICE

The benefits of using a Bible-size notebook or an electronic device for personal organization are well established. Many companies have developed products for this purpose. So why am I talking about it? Because it works. It's also biblical to be organized. First Corinthians 14:40 says, "Let all things be done decently and in order." I realize that people can be organized without a retrieval system, but most of us need a little help.

Someone once said, "One of the greatest hindrances to doing God's will is the lack of planning." For the speaker, the lack of planning can be disastrous. The memory of the time I realized, too late, that I had accepted two major speaking engagements for the same day is still too fresh for comfort! I had no one to blame but myself. It was a matter of keeping poor records.

I was impressed recently when I read a comment George Whitefield made when he was asked what he would do if he knew Christ would return in three days. He replied, "I would do just what I have scheduled to do."

My organizer has helped to keep me scheduled and prepared. Customize a notebook or an electronic system for yourself—one that's small enough to take with you almost everywhere. Here are some suggestions for index tabs/sections within a notebook/organizer that work well for speakers.

Daily To-Do List

The first section of my notebook is devoted to keeping me on target daily. I put today's date on the page and list everything I need to accomplish —phone calls to return, letters to answer, household tasks, trips to the bank or the cleaners, and so on. I mark off each item as I deal with it. I'm an inveterate list maker, so if I accomplish anything of merit during the day that was not on my list, I write it down for the sheer pleasure of drawing a line through it. At the conclusion of the day, I check the list. If there are any items left, I write them on the page for the next day. I never live in the past; I throw out each day's sheet at the end of that day.

Calendar

My calendar comes next because I refer to it often during the day. I like month-at-a-glance calendars. When someone calls me for a weekend speaking engagement, with one glance I can see how many weekends in a row I'm scheduling and if it looks like I'd be overcommitted to take one more for that month. I circle dates that are scheduled for speaking engagements, and I underline dates that are reserved for family and friends. Claim the days you want to be home ahead of time. (More on that topic in the next chapter.)

Prayer List

I have a different prayer list for every day of the week. It allows me to pray specifically for individuals and to let them know that "Wednesday is my prayer day for you." By rotating the names of various family members, missionaries, and friends, and praying for them on separate days, my prayer life stays fresh and vibrant. Sometimes I give close friends a sheet out of my notebook and ask them to list specific ways they would like to be remembered in prayer. This has added a significant, intimate dimension to my prayer life.

Journal

My journal sheets come next. I don't write every day, but I do record my thoughts several times a week. This is where I write my response to what I've read in the Bible, where I answer the question, *What does this mean to me?* Sometimes I write out prayers to the Lord. I reflect on people I've interacted with during the day, emotions I felt, fears I experienced, excitement I encountered, challenges that came my way, and many other things. For a speaker, a journal is extremely valuable because you will get many ideas for illustrations from it. Be sure to date your entries. One benefit of having your journal in a notebook is that you can easily remove the pages and file them in a private place.

Sermon and Conference Notes

This is usually the largest section of my notebook. As a speaker steps on the podium, I write down the name and date the page. No matter how poor the delivery might be, I take notes. Why? Because I critique speakers in seminars all the time, and it would be far too easy for me to judge the delivery instead of listening to the content. It's a matter of personal discipline, and the wonderful surprise is that when I listen for the content of the message, there's *always* something of value to remember. When this section of my notebook gets weighty, I remove the pages and file the notes in my Genesis through Revelation files or in my topical files.

Expenses

When you come to the point of receiving honorariums and travel expenses for your speaking engagements, keep careful records. The Internal Revenue Service requires you to keep track of your mileage and expenses as well as your income. In the beginning days of speaking, you may find that your expenses outweigh your income, but you are getting a wonderful education as you speak for "less than you're worth," and you are learning how to do the record keeping that will be important as your ministry multiplies.

Miscellaneous

Into this section goes everything that is necessary to my daily organization that doesn't fit anywhere else. Frequently used phone numbers and addresses are here. I keep a record of the clothing sizes of my family, so if I'm out of town and find a good sale, I can make economical purchases at that time.

Purchase a notebook that has a storage place for personal stationery, stamps, and a pen. It's a great time saver to have those items with you when you are waiting for an appointment. This tool has enhanced my outward efficiency more than anything else.

ANSWER THE MAIL EFFICIENTLY

Handle unimportant mail only once. Don't read junk mail twice just to make sure that you want to throw it away. If it's still on your desk, you'll waste too many minutes on trivia. When it's appropriate, answer mail electronically.

Mark your business mail (including printed e-mail) with a contrasting pen as you read it. Mark any information on the *place* of a speaking engagement, the *time*, the *theme*, the *directions* to the meeting place, and any *requests* for information from you. This will keep you from having to reread the entire letter when you answer it or when you need to record important details about the engagement.

Pile your mail under "Personal" or "Ministry." Take the "Ministry" pile, and priority rank it from top to bottom before you start answering the letters. This will keep you from overwhelming guilt about not answering the urgent mail when you are short on time.

Include everything the other party may need in your first correspondence. This could include your promotional information, picture, request for directions, travel and overnight arrangements—whatever pertains to your date with that group. Sometimes inexperienced retreat or conference leaders don't know what to ask you for, and they send five or six e-mails requesting different information with each note. It can be very time consuming for you to respond to all of this correspondence for one engagement. You can tactfully help a new leader and save yourself a lot of grief by wording your first e-mail/letter well.

Follow up with a postcard if necessary. When you accept an engagement many months ahead of the scheduled date, often the paperwork is done, and there is no reason to be in touch with the chairperson. It's comforting to that person to receive your note saying that you are looking forward to being at the conference next week. It will also enhance your image as a thoughtful, organized speaker.

Write two personal letters or e-notes of encouragement daily. This is my goal on every at-home day. The more you travel as a speaker, the more important it becomes to foster close ties with those who support you and love you. Your life is often consumed with the urgent, and you need to make time for the important — but that's what the next chapter is all about!

REMEMBER THIS THOUGHT

I can't take credit for saying it first, but it's very true: "All of us have 168 hours each week. We sleep about 56 hours (8 times 7), and use approximately 12 hours for personal hygiene. That leaves 100 hours a week for you to plan. How are you choosing to use those hours?"

PART SIX

Where Do I Go from Here?

THIRTEEN

Disciplines of the Effective Speaker

The Difference Between "Doing" and "Being"

*What were we made for? To know God. What aim should we
set ourselves in life? To know God. What is the best thing in
life, bringing more joy, delight, and contentment than anything
else? Knowledge of God. . . . Once you become aware that the
main business that you are here for is to know God, most of
life's problems fall into place of their own accord.*[1]

—J. I. PACKER

Rain and hail pelted the windshield of the car, blurring my view of the road. I was exhausted after a full day—a day that consisted of a 4:00 a.m. wake-up call, a four-hour drive to a retreat location, three keynote messages, and lots of interaction with people. I still had a four-hour drive home—four hours, that is, in good weather.

My head was announcing the onslaught of a migraine. I kept remembering that when I did get home, I had to prepare for another engagement the next day. All of this looked easy when it stared at me from the neat, orderly pages of my calendar. *Living* through my commitments was another story!

Tears flooded my eyes, adding to my vision problem. I hadn't counted on the delay. Guilt over being an absentee mother too much during the week was making my load heavier. Pulling into a truck stop, I loosened my seat belt and lay on the front seat sobbing. I wanted to be home—not here! After wallowing in self-pity for a few more minutes,

I prayed, "Lord, I'm trying to be a five-talent person in a two-talent body. I can't do it anymore!"

PRIORITIES

My mind went back to a scene from the week before. I had jumped out of bed early, showered, dressed hurriedly, and sat reading the paper at the kitchen table while enjoying a freshly brewed cup of coffee.

J.P. came downstairs a few minutes later. I made him some breakfast and returned to my coffee. Minutes later while peering at me over his cereal bowl, he said, "Mama, you look so pretty today."

I couldn't believe it. On most days I'm quite dressed up—always a bit more comfortable in business attire than in a pair of blue jeans and sneakers. On the day in question, I had dressed for leisure—nothing special, just slacks and a sweater.

We made eye contact, and I questioned him: "Honey, why do you think I look pretty today? These are old clothes, and usually Mother's wearing something nicer."

He flashed his gorgeous blue eyes and smiled at me. "It's because," he said thoughtfully, "when you're all dressed up, I know you're going out some place, but when you look like this, I know you're all mine!"

His answer was like an arrow, piercing my heart and pinning me to the back of the chair. It had never dawned on me that this little boy could tell if I had *time* for him by what I was wearing on any given day.

While sitting in the parking lot waiting for the storm to let up, I thought about my own mother and dad. Dad always had time to take us for Sunday afternoon walks. It wasn't until I grew up that I realized those walks were planned more for *talking* than for walking! Dad taught me by word and example that the important things in life are not prestige or money. To this day the things he values most are knowing God and doing His will.

And what about Mother? In years past, she'd gather the six of us in an armlock and have prayer at the door before we left for school—

every day. Mom is an early riser, and I would often peer down from the big open stairs and see her on her knees, praying out loud for her kids, by name.

She prayed for us while we were in the womb, and she started early praying for our future spouses. She figured they were alive somewhere and could use the prayer as God prepared them to marry her children. When Mother ironed dresses for her five daughters (before the days of wrinkle-free fabrics), she prayed for the little girls who would wear those dresses. She did the same for Dad and my brother, Ben, when she laundered their shirts.

A short time ago I was reflecting on my heritage and jotted down some thoughts about Mother. The notes were in my car, and I pulled them out and read:

My mother has never written a book or spoken to large crowds of people. She was never interviewed on the radio or featured in a Christian women's magazine. Mother has not had the privilege of going to a university or holding a fancy title for her work in God's kingdom.

"What *did* your mother do?" you ask.

Mother gave birth to six children, over a span of seventeen years. Every day, without fail, she read Bible stories and Christian biographies to us. We memorized the books of the Bible and Scripture verses as a part of daily life. And we never realized, until many years later, how much we had learned at Mother's knee.

Mother was rarely in a noticeable rush. She always had time to listen; she was never too busy for a word of prayer and a comforting hug. Mother made all six of us know, beyond any doubt, that individually, we were her favorite child!

As I finished reading, I realized that the hail had stopped, but the rain was still beating mercilessly on the car. There was something about the gloom of the weather that seemed appropriate when combined with my melancholy mood. I wondered what my son would remember about his home and family in years to come. Would he recall a mom who was always rushing off to a speaking engagement, or would he remember the family devotions, the celebrations, the singing, the laughter, the vacations, the traditions, the guests in our home, the books we read, and the prayer times together?

There was a special sense of God's presence in the car, and that day a truck stop in northern Indiana became hallowed ground. It was impossible to kneel properly, but I placed myself in subjection to my Lord and prayed, "Father, I have sinned. Forgive me for allowing spiritual activities and ministry opportunities to take precedence over my personal relationship with You and my care of the most important people in my life. Teach me the balance between *knowing* You and *serving* You."

Have you ever experienced what I've been describing? The formula is not complex. You start by accepting your quota of speaking engagements for a given week—your "quota" being what you know you can handle while simultaneously maintaining personal priorities. Then someone calls and asks if you're free to speak for a group on a specific day of that week, on one of the days already reserved for home and family.

Most of the time, it's easy to say no. But if the engagement is prestigious (important enough that your ego is inflated by the invitation) or if friends are asking for your services, that's another story. More often than not, you agree to something you don't really have time for because of pride or pressure. When you live through a week like that, it's easy to feel like a Christian martyr instead of accepting responsibility for your own overcommitment.

In one of his letters, C. S. Lewis admonished a friend,

> Don't be too easily convinced that God really wants you to do all sorts of work you needn't do. Each must do his duty "in that state of life to which God has called him." . . . There can be intemperance in work just as in drink. What feels like

zeal may be only fidgets or even the flattering of one's self-importance. As MacDonald says, "In holy things may be unholy greed." And by doing what "one's station and its duties" does not demand, one can make oneself less fit for the duties it does demand and so commit some injustice. Just you give Mary a little chance as well as Martha![2]

PROBLEMS

Lewis was right. There is a vast difference between *doing* and *being*. When I take on more than I should, everything in my life is affected.

My relationship with God suffers. There's not enough time for in-depth Bible study and prayer. I'm too busy "ministering to the masses" to remember that my most important mission in life is to know God.

My relationships with family members become strained. I'm so involved with preparing to serve Jesus that I make the people closest to me feel that they are intruding on my precious time. Subtly, the impression is given that my work for God is more important than them.

Friends quit calling. They've asked me to go to lunch on so many occasions when I was unavailable that they've stopped trying. When I'm overcommitted in ministry, I shut out the people I need the most.

Sharp words come out of my mouth—nothing immoral, just communication that is unfeeling, tactless, and short. After all, I have places to go and people to see.

My home takes on "hidden" disorganization. I'm the kind of person who cares a lot about what people think. That means if you drop by unexpectedly, it would *appear* that I have everything under control. However, if you check the drawers, the closets, and the hideaway places, you'd find clutter and chaos.

My office door is closed. When this happens, I'm in the danger zone and sinking fast! Files are misplaced. Unanswered mail is stacked all over the desk. Seminar supplies are stashed along the wall. Newspapers and magazines are in a pile on the floor waiting to be read. When I can't find my computer keyboard under this mess, an internal siren goes off in my head, warning me of impending doom.

Some of you are saying, "But, Carol, this doesn't apply to me. I'm reading this book because I need help in *developing* my ability to speak. I don't have this problem."

Overcommitment in the life of the speaker never begins overnight. It starts as innocent, exciting, fulfilling opportunity. Slowly, as more and more doors for ministry open, there is a growing flattery of one's own self-importance. As a speaker, you may be made to feel that you are the *only* appropriate choice for special conventions and conferences. Many groups work their dates around when you are available, feeding your self-esteem and subtly enticing you to fill every available space on the calendar.

Abruptly, you come to a crisis point, as I did on the day of the storm. There is the sudden realization that the engagements that started out as joy-filled opportunities to serve the Lord have become beasts of burden. You have allowed yourself to be controlled by other people's demands and your own unconquerable ego. You're trapped! You never noticed the creeping cancer of overcommitment in the early stages. Now it's attacking your vital organs.

PRINCIPLES

I work at my favorite hobby. God has given me a love for people and a desire to communicate practical, biblical, life-changing principles to others. Most of the time the joy I experience in ministry is beyond description. It's only when I allow pride or pressure to coerce me into overcommitment that I have big problems.

In his best-selling book *Ordering Your Private World*, Gordon MacDonald shares observations on the life of Christ:

When I look into the Bible, I am deeply impressed with the practical lessons on organization that one can learn from the life and work of Jesus Christ. . . . It would appear that He lived with very much the same sort of intrusions and demands with which we are familiar. But one never gets the feeling when studying the life of Christ that He ever hurried, that He ever had to play "catch up ball," or that He was ever taken by surprise. Not only was He adept at handling His public time without an appointments secretary, He managed adequate amounts of time alone for the purpose of prayer and meditation, and for being with the few He had gathered around Him for the purpose of discipleship. . . . He knew His sense of mission. . . . It was never difficult for Him to say a firm no to invitations and demands which might have looked good or acceptable to us.[3]

As we consider these thoughts, let's discuss some practical principles.

1. Make knowing God your highest aim.

Thus says the LORD:
> "Let not the wise man glory in his wisdom,
> Let not the mighty man glory in his might,
> Nor let the rich man glory in his riches;
> But let him who glories glory in this,
> That he understands and knows Me,
> That I am the LORD, exercising lovingkindness, judgment,
and righteousness in the earth.
> For in these I delight," says the LORD. (Jeremiah 9:23-24)

When my top priority is to understand and know Him, the activities of my life do not control me. In Mark 1:21-35, we see twenty-four hours in the life of Jesus. In this time period Jesus was involved in teaching (verses 21-22), healing (verses 23-27), visiting a shut-in (verses 29-31), ministering to "the whole city" (verses 32-34), and taking time alone for meditation and prayer (verse 35). It is instantly apparent that time alone with His Father was the priority of His life that kept the rest of His ministry on target, even on the busiest of days.

2. Learn to say no. In January of 1982 I was in Austin, Texas, and sat under the ministry of Dr. Alan Redpath for several days. It was a rich time in the Word, and one thing the beloved teacher said became a foundation stone of my personal discipline.

All of us in the audience were Bible study teachers with many demands on our time. He looked at us with a penetrating gaze and said, "Say yes to the burden that God puts on your heart and say no to everything else."

What a great way to plan a schedule! Instead of committing myself to every invitation that comes along, I stop to consider some questions: Do I feel pressured to accept this ministry opportunity because *people* are putting a burden on me? Am I tempted to accept this engagement primarily because it's a *flattering ego trip* to say yes to this one? Do I have a *God-given urgency* to be involved in serving the Lord in that place?

It was a freeing experience to learn to say no. I found out that God has others. I wasn't the only person who could fill the need for a speaker. Because I recommended other people who were well-qualified but not yet well-known speakers, ministry expanded for them, and I had the fulfillment of being an encourager in their lives.

The unexpected benefit was that I had calendar space left to say yes to opportunities that *were* the burden of my heart. I had more quality time with my family, and I was rested enough to minister with great energy and enthusiasm, free of the guilt that accompanies overcommitment.

3. Realize that public ministry is not more important than other service for God. When did we begin equating spiritual success with the limelight? My spirituality has nothing to do with how many books I write in my lifetime or how many air miles I log this year in Christian service.

Ruth Harms Calkins captures the essence of this truth in one of her poems. It's appropriately titled "Sad Facsimile."

> Lord, I am ashamed!
> Too often I have asked You
> To do whatever You wish with me.
> But I am never quite content
> Unless You wish to make of me
> Something flattering
> Something spectacular
> Something colorful and praiseworthy
> For all the world to see.
> What a sad facsimile
> Of genuine spirituality.[4]

4. Expect criticism. If you serve the Lord in a public ministry, you will be criticized at some point. Be prepared for it, realizing you are in very good company. The Bible is full of examples of godly people who endured ridicule and abuse. In Jesus' first public teaching ministry, the Sermon on the Mount, one of the teachings He gave was this: "Blessed are those who are persecuted for righteousness' sake, for theirs is the kingdom of heaven" (Matthew 5:10).

In much of the world today people are being physically persecuted for the cause of Christ. For the most part, malicious gossip and unjust criticism are all we have to endure in America. By comparison, it seems a small price to pay for ministry—unless you happen to be the one going through it. Remember Paul's advice when hard times come: "We are hard-pressed on every side, yet not crushed; we are perplexed, but not in despair; persecuted, but not forsaken; struck down, but not destroyed" (2 Corinthians 4:8-9).

When criticism comes, think about the following questions: Is it true (even part of it)? Does anything need to change in my personal life or ministry? What is my attitude, and how can the work of God be furthered by my response to this situation?

All of this sounds wonderful on paper, but living through it can be another matter. A few years ago I received a phone call from a speaker friend. After we talked for a while, she tactfully relayed a criticism that had been passed on to her regarding my ministry. Convinced that it wasn't true, she encouraged me to get in touch with the person who was misinformed so the problem could be cleared up.

The "problem" was that a retreat director in another state thought she heard me use a four-letter word on a recording of my message titled "Learning to Be a Lover, a Biblical Approach to Physical Intimacy." I was devastated! The word in question wasn't even in my thought life and had never been in my ministry. Because intimacy in marriage is such a delicate subject, I had carefully worded every part of that talk. There were letters in my files from ministers, thanking me for that same message and complimenting me on handling a difficult subject in a tasteful, Bible-based manner. Hundreds of copies of that talk had been in circulation for over two years, and this was the first complaint.

My initial reaction was to curl up in the fetal position and quit speaking. I wanted to hide under a big blanket and close out the whole world. I began to think of all the negative possibilities. If my friend had heard this, how many other people knew of this and were wondering about me? Had leaders in other states been told to "watch out for Carol Kent"? For two days I didn't answer the phone. I had been misunderstood, and the pain was so great I didn't feel like talking to anyone.

Once the initial hurt began to subside, I wanted to write a letter and give the woman in question a piece of my mind. How *could* she suggest something like that without ever having met me? If she was so sure I had "done the deed," couldn't she have called and confronted me? I began to understand part of God's plan in allowing us the experience of deep hurt. My pain kept me from writing while I was still angry, and it allowed me the time necessary to see the situation from a different perspective.

The woman wasn't malicious. Perhaps a word had been slurred

in high-speed duplication. Maybe she hadn't listened to the CD long enough to realize that the word she *thought* she heard wouldn't fit the context of the message. I began to give her the benefit of the doubt, and I prayed that God would help me write a letter that would allow her to see her mistake and still be able to face me with dignity.

One of the important points to remember when you go through unjust criticism is this: Pray *before* you react. Perhaps someone sincerely misunderstood your material, method, or motive. Sincere misunderstanding was the culprit in the situation I have just described. I wrote to the woman, and within a short time I received a lovely letter from her thanking me for contacting her and clearing up the problem. Proverbs 12:18 says, "Reckless words pierce like a sword, but the tongue of the wise brings healing" (NIV).

Don't forget that once a rumor has "gone to the wind," you can't undo everything. When you bear the brunt of an untruth, it's hard to maintain your spiritual perspective. Just remember that Satan is the author of confusion, and he must believe your work is effective enough to be worthy of his time and attention! (Small consolation, but worth thinking about.)

5. Plan for celebration and sabbath. One year I sat in an audience and listened to John Bertrand tell his story. He was the skipper for the *Australia II* and led his crew to victory over the America's Cup defender, *Liberty*, in September of 1983, thus ending a 132-year winning streak by the Americans. His story had it all—drama, excitement, adventure, intrigue, and video clips of the win.

He said, "We wanted to become the best in the world, and we needed a sense of pride." The Australians began working hard on building that pride, starting with their flag. It was a green flag with a kangaroo on it. The new design was still green, but they put red boxing gloves on the kangaroo and flew it only when they won.

Next, they needed a battle hymn. They were given a great song and bought the largest speakers they could find. Whenever they left the dock or came back in, the battle hymn was played with the volume turned up.

They made a confident statement about their potential in the race!

Finally, they needed a winning edge, a technical advantage that would give their crew hope and would keep the opponent guessing. We all know the story of their controversial keel design. They kept it covered until the race started, adding to the opponent's anxiety. When the *Australia II* crossed the finish line first, Mr. Bertrand said the celebrations in his homeland were similar to those at the end of World War II.

Two weeks after the win, the skipper was back home speaking in front of five hundred elementary school children, telling of his adventure and showing the video clips. When the presentation was finished, he volunteered to answer any questions. A little boy queried, "Mr. Bertrand, while you were in America, did you see any butterflies?"

What a profound question for speakers as well as for skippers! Reaching our goal takes an enormous amount of energy and preparation. We aren't working with flags, battle hymns, and keels, but we *are* working with outlines, illustrations, and applications. I'm sure there is a temptation for the great sailor to live from race to race. Certainly for the speaker, there is a temptation to live from one speaking engagement to the next. If you're not speaking, you're preparing for the next one.

It's a sad day when you discover that you rarely take time for celebrations with family and friends anymore. Most people in this category don't plan for rest periods (sabbaths), either. Life goes by very quickly, and you wake up one day to realize you haven't seen any butterflies in a long time.

Our family plans ahead for "butterfly time." My husband and I get our calendars together, and often as far as a year in advance, we seize the days that we are claiming for ourselves. We plan gatherings in our home for family and friends. We decide on vacation weeks and "down time" when we can physically and mentally relax. When we work, we work very hard; when we play, we play hard.

Right now, during my writing of this manuscript, I'm in a work mode, sometimes researching and writing for twelve hours a day. It's not always fun to sit at my desk until an idea comes. I'd rather go to the beach or plan a picnic. But this is chapter 13, and next month our family is celebrating! Hard work makes celebration and sabbath even more wonderful—plan for it!

6. Have prayer partners. Years ago R. A. Torrey said, "Pray for great things, expect great things, work for great things, but above all, pray." I have long believed in the necessity of prayer for power in ministry.

In my beginning days of speaking I often requested prayer for specific ministry times at the Wednesday night service in my church. As God expanded my opportunities to travel as a speaker, it occurred to me that perhaps there was a better way to obtain prayer for ministry.

There were two problems. First, requesting prayer for a speaking engagement in sunny Florida when it's freezing in Michigan can be wrongly perceived. To the woman stuck at home with five children who hasn't had a vacation in that many years, it sounded as if I were headed for an exotic vacation. The person who travels very little may not understand the exhaustion and pressure of working on the road.

Second, and more important, requesting public prayer for speaking engagements that involved large groups or major trips was a way of telling my home folks how popular I was and how well known I had become. It was one big ego trip and definitely not the right reason for requesting prayer.

The Lord impressed upon me that He was fully capable of laying the burden of prayer for this ministry on the hearts of those He wanted to pray for it. Within two weeks eight people had individually come to me and asked for the privilege of regularly and consistently praying for my ministry. Others have contacted me over the years, and God continues to add to this group.

My parents do the collating of the materials for the notebooks used in the Speak Up seminar. Because of the index tabs, these materials cannot be machine collated. As time goes on, the efficiency of that job has been improved, but I'll never forget the day Mother and Dad came to my home to work on the first three hundred notebooks. The place looked like a warehouse—boxes all over and piles of individual sheets in a line from the dining room table and buffet to the kitchen counter and around to the kitchen table and then to two chairs and a bookshelf. What an assembly line!

Leaving Mom and Dad in charge, I went to my desk and answered several pieces of correspondence. Two hours later I looked in on them. There they were, walking around in snakelike fashion, picking up each sheet and then moving on to the next pile. Realizing how time consuming and arduous the task was, I said, "Mom and Dad, why don't I hire some teenagers to do this job? It's just too much work, and it takes too long."

Mom smiled and looked at me for a moment. "Carol," she said, "you will never know what a privilege it is for me to do this. While I've been picking up the contents of these notebooks, I've been praying for the people who will use them and for their families and ministries. Every time I pick up the page with your picture on it, I've been praying for you, that God will use you as a vehicle for His message as you teach and speak."

The secret to success in ministry is not a streamlined program or a dynamic presentation. Yes, I believe God uses education. He expects us to get prepared to serve Him with excellence, and He holds us accountable for what we do with our training. *But God moves in hearts as people pray.*

Many individuals have committed themselves to prayer regarding the writing of this manuscript. If anything in this book has made a difference in your life and ministry, it isn't because the author did a good job. It's because of the prayer that has gone into this project. When you prepare your messages, don't forget the most important ingredient.

7. Provide a pattern for others. The woman looked at me over her half-glasses and asked, "Who takes care of your son when you're away speaking?"

I didn't like the tone of her voice, and her whole approach was triggering a negative reaction. In one of my baser moments, I was tempted to respond with a sarcastic remark. Thankfully, the comment didn't make it past the thought stage, and I tactfully responded, telling her that my husband is self-employed and that he works his appointment schedule around J.P.'s school hours when I'm away.

In my early days of speaking I always expected people to be spiritually mature enough to realize that ministering away from home is difficult and that no concerned Christian wife and mother would ever do it if life on the home front was not taken care of first. I've mellowed a bit in the last few years and realize that people are curious about my family. More than that, they genuinely want to know that my house is in order before I teach the Bible to them.

I have come to the conclusion that my audiences deserve an honest accounting of my home life. Paul said, "Dear brothers and sisters, pattern your lives after mine, and learn from those who follow our example" (Philippians 3:17, NLT). He continued in Titus 2:7, "In all things showing yourself to be a pattern." The wording used in 1 Corinthians 4:16 is even stronger: "Therefore I urge you, imitate me."

The dictionary defines a *pattern* as "a person or thing so ideal as to be worthy of imitation." Every audience wants to know that your lifestyle is backing up what you say you believe.

Tim Hansel eloquently states this principle in capsule form: "All of our theology must eventually become biography. The constant challenge in this life we call Christian is the translation of all we believe to be true into our day-to-day lifestyle."[5] For people like Tim, that means living a joyful Christian life in a body racked with constant physical pain, a result of a mountain-climbing accident. For me as a speaker, it means being transparent enough to allow people to know that the principles I teach are the same principles I live by. That was easier before my son was arrested for a serious crime.

Francis Schaeffer stated,

No work of art is more important than the Christian's own life, and every Christian is called upon to be an artist in this sense. He may have no gift of writing, no gift of composing or singing, but each man has the gift of creativity in terms of the way he lives his life.[6]

The question is this: Are you providing others with a Christlike pattern that is worthy of imitation?

PRACTICE

Throughout this book, I've outlined principles for speaking up with confidence. Now it's your turn to put this material into practice. When you've done your homework and have opportunities to teach and speak, you will be greatly exhilarated when people comment: "You're the best speaker we've ever had!" "This Bible study would fall apart if you weren't our teacher." "Your message changed my life." When that happens, remember one of Dr. A. W. Tozer's stories:

> It's the first Palm Sunday, and here comes Jesus riding into Jerusalem on a donkey. The crowds begin to shout "Hosanna! Hosanna!" The old donkey pricks up his ears. Some in the crowd throw their coats in the road; others spread out palm branches.
>
> "Well!" says the donkey, switching a fly off a mange patch. "I had no idea they really appreciated me like this! Listen to those hosannas, would you. I must really be something!"[7]

My friends, if anybody says to you, "Wow! You're fantastic! What a communicator!" just remember that all you did was to bring Jesus to them.

For information on how you can attend a Speak Up with Confidence seminar in your area, or for a list of resources available through Carol Kent's ministry, go to:

www.CarolKent.org

888.860.7719

810.982.0898 (outside USA)

Notes

Chapter One: **Speak? Not Me!**
1. Henry David Thoreau, quoted in *Familiar Quotations*, ed. John Bartlett (Boston: Little, Brown, 1980), 559.

Chapter Two: **Moses, Me, and Other Unlikely Public Speakers**
1. Richard Rothe, quoted in the *Leadership Desk Calendar*, week of November 3-9, 1986.
2. An insightful character study of Miriam can be found in the book *Passionate Faith* by Jennie Afman Dimkoff, Fleming H. Revell, 2005, chapter 3.
3. Bob Benson, *Come Share the Being*, copyrighted by Generoux Publishing Group, division of Solitude & Celebration Press, 5039 Hillsboro Road #167, Nashville, Tennessee 37215. Used by permission.

Chapter Three:
If You Don't Know Where You're Going, You'll Probably Wind Up Somewhere Else
1. Tim Timmons, "Why Should They Listen to Me?" *Leadership* 6, no. 4 (Fall 1985): 88. Used by permission.
2. François de Sales, quoted in the *Leadership Desk Calendar*, week of April 28–May 4, 1986.

3. Many of the outlines in this chapter were developed by Bonnie Emmorey, Speaker Coach and Trainer, www .SpeakUpSpeakerServices.com.

Chapter Four: **Big Lips and Other Beauty Marks**

1. Old Arab proverb, quoted by Mark R. Littleton, "Raisins in the Oatmeal: The Art of Illustrating Sermons," *Leadership* 4, no. 2 (Spring 1983): 66.

Chapter Five: **Start with a Bang!**

1. Russian proverb, quoted by Haddon W. Robinson, *Biblical Preaching* (Grand Rapids, MI: Baker, 1980), 160.
2. Paul O'Neil, quoted by Robinson, 161–162. Used by permission.
3. William Fry, quoted in *USA Today*, December 16, 1983. Reprinted with permission.
4. Denis Waitley and Reni L. Witt, *The Joy of Working* (New York: Dodd, Mead, 1985), 18–19.
5. Marilyn Elias, "When We Chuckle, We Show More Than Our Smiles," *USA Today*, December 16, 1983. Reprinted with permission.
6. Kenneth S. Kantzer, "In Search of Heroes," *Christianity Today*, 30, no. 16 (November 8, 1985): 16–17. Used by permission.

Chapter Six: **Finishing Touches**

1. Bill Bright, quoted in *Great Quotes and Illustrations*, comp. George Sweeting (Waco, TX: Word, 1985), 201.
2. Alan H. Monroe, *Principles and Types of Speech* (Chicago: Scott Foresman and Co., 1962), 268.
3. Charles R. Swindoll, *Growing Strong in the Seasons of Life* (Portland, OR: Multnomah, 1983), 94–95.
4. Alan Redpath, *Blessings Out of Buffetings* (Old Tappan, NJ: Revell, 1965), 60.

5. William F. Hobby, quoted by Mary Bray Wheeler, gen. ed., *The Basic Meeting Manual* (Nashville: Thomas Nelson, 1986), 189.
6. Hobby, 190.
7. William E. Sangster, quoted by Haddon W. Robinson, *Biblical Preaching* (Grand Rapids, MI: Baker, 1980), 172. Used by permission.

Chapter Seven: **Little Things Mean a Lot**

1. Haddon W. Robinson, *Biblical Preaching* (Grand Rapids, MI: Baker, 1980), 202-203.
2. Robinson, 203.
3. Gerard I. Nierenberg and Henry H. Calero, *How to Read a Person Like a Book* (New York: Hawthorn Books, 1971), reprinted by permission of Dutton Signet, a division of Penguin Books USA Inc.
4. Julius Fast, *Body Language* (New York: M. Evans and Company, 1970). Reprinted by permission.
5. Alan H. Monroe, *Principles and Types of Speech* (Chicago: Scott Foresman and Co., 1962), 54.
6. J. W. Peterson, "Heaven Came Down and Glory Filled My Soul" (Scottsdale, AZ: J. W. Peterson Music Co., 1961). Used by permission.
7. Nierenberg and Calero, 41.

Chapter Eight: **Pursue Excellence**

1. John W. Gardner, quoted in *Great Quotes and Illustrations*, comp. George Sweeting (Waco, TX: Word, 1985), 108.
2. Haddon W. Robinson, *Biblical Preaching* (Grand Rapids, MI: Baker, 1980), 196.
3. John T. Molloy, *Dress for Success* (New York: Warner Books, 1975), 121.
4. S. Truett Cathy, *Leadership* 7, no. 3 (Summer 1986): 35.

Chapter Nine: **Getting Started**

1. Dwight Eisenhower, quoted in *Quotable Quotations*, comp. Lloyd Cory (Wheaton, IL: Victor Books, 1985), 211.
2. Jack Herbert, quoted in *Quotable Quotations*, 363.
3. Mary Bray Wheeler, gen. ed., *The Basic Meeting Manual* (Nashville: Thomas Nelson, 1986), 211.
4. For information on dates and locations of Speak Up with Confidence seminars, go to www.CarolKent.org and click on Seminars.

Chapter Ten: **Your Life Story Has Potential!**

1. Francis Schaeffer, quoted in *Great Quotes and Illustrations*, comp. George Sweeting (Waco, TX: Word, 1985), 130.
2. Mrs. Howard Taylor, *The Triumph of John and Betty Stam* (Chicago: Moody, 1935), 126.
3. A. Wetherell Johnson, *Created for Commitment* (Wheaton, IL: Tyndale, 1982). Used by permission.

Chapter Eleven: **The Most Exciting Book of All!**

1. R. C. Sproul, *Knowing Scripture* (Downers Grove, IL: InterVarsity, 1977), 23.
2. Earl Radmacher, quoted from a message given at Maranatha Bible Conference, Muskegon, Michigan, August 22, 1985.
3. Radmacher.
4. Sproul, 64–65.
5. "How Great Thou Art," © Copyright 1953 S. K. Hine. Assigned to Manna Music, Inc., 35255 Brooten Road, Pacific City, OR 97135. Renewed 1981. All Rights Reserved. Used by permission. (ASCAP)
6. Haddon W. Robinson, *Biblical Preaching* (Grand Rapids, MI: Baker, 1980), 18–19.
7. Arthur W. Pink, *Exposition of the Gospel of John* (Grand Rapids, MI: Zondervan, 1976), 242.

8. Ideas for this outline are from a message given by Alan Redpath in Austin, Texas, January 1982.
9. Redpath.

Chapter Twelve: **Organization — Inside and Out**

1. Alan Lakein, quoted by Mark Less, *How to Set Goals and Really Reach Them* (Portland, OR: Horizon House, 1978), 179.
2. C. S. Lewis, *Mere Christianity* (Westwood, NJ: Barbour, 1952), 173.
3. www.familyfirstaid.org.

Chapter Thirteen: **Disciplines of the Effective Speaker**

1. J. I. Packer, *Knowing God* (Downers Grove, IL: InterVarsity, 1973), 129.
2. C. S. Lewis, *Letters to an American Lady* (Grand Rapids, MI: Eerdmans, 1967), 50–51.
3. Gordon MacDonald, *Ordering Your Private World* (Nashville: Oliver-Nelson, 1984), 74–78.
4. Ruth Harms Calkins, *Lord, It Keeps Happening and Happening* (Wheaton, IL: Tyndale, 1984).
5. Tim Hansel, *You Gotta Keep Dancin'* (Elgin, IL: David C. Cook, 1985), 41.
6. Francis Schaeffer, quoted in *Worldwide Challenge* 12, no. 6 (November-December 1985), back cover.
7. A. W. Tozer, quoted by Anne Ortlund, *Up With Worship* (Glendale, CA: Regal, 1975), 119–120.

Recommended Reading List

Author's note: The absence of any of your favorite reference books from this list means nothing. These suggestions are based on my current library, which is continuously being updated and enlarged. The purpose of this reading list is not to be exhaustive in nature but to suggest a starting point for the reader who needs a place to begin.

Spiritual Priorities

Elliot, Elisabeth. *Discipline: The Glad Surrender.* Grand Rapids, MI: Baker/Revell, 2006. A serious book for people who desire to say yes to discipline, commitment, and obedience.

Foster, Richard J. *Celebration of Discipline.* San Francisco: Harper & Row, 1998. A book that must be cut up into bite-sized pieces, chewed until the full flavor activates the spiritual senses, and then swallowed, even if one did not order or desire the entrée. Contains a controversial chapter on meditation, but is still an important book.

Johnson, A. Wetherell. *Created for Commitment.* Wheaton, IL: Tyndale, 1982. The remarkable biography of the founder of Bible Study Fellowship. To study this woman's life is to understand what spiritual discipline means.

Johnson, Jan. *Enjoying the Presence of God*. Colorado Springs, CO: NavPress, 1996. A book that offers simple, tangible insights into practicing God's presence. Includes a wealth of quotations from classic Christian writers.

Kent, Carol. *Secret Longings of the Heart*. Colorado Springs, CO: NavPress, 1990. This book emphasizes the need to develop a biblical belief system as we long for significance, security, intimacy, success, and spirituality.

Lucado, Max. *In the Grip of Grace*. Dallas: Word, 1996. A reminder that the God who first made us is strong enough to sustain us. Any speaker or leader who struggles with fear will benefit.

MacDonald, Gordon. *Ordering Your Private World*. Nashville, TN: Oliver-Nelson, 1984. "Wingers" will benefit greatly from MacDonald's "Memo to the Disorganized." His "Laws of Unseized Time" challenge the reader to squeeze productive moments out of wasted leisure.

Packer, J. I. *Knowing God*. Downers Grove, IL: InterVarsity, 1993. Not a reference book per se, but essential for understanding the nature, attributes, and majesty of God Almighty.

Sanders, J. Oswald. *Spiritual Leadership*. Chicago: Moody, 1994. Should be required reading for the Christian leader. Contains many reusable quotes and illustrations, but the primary value is the challenge to accept the privilege and responsibility of leadership.

Swindoll, Charles R. *Intimacy with the Almighty*. Dallas: Word, 1996, 2000. For leaders who long to become more deeply and intimately acquainted with Christ.

Illustrations and Quotations

Bartlett, John, ed. *Bartlett's Familiar Quotations.* Boston: Little, Brown, 1992. With more than 20,000 quotations, representing 2,550 authors, this new sixteenth edition is a necessity for the serious speaker.

Heald, Cynthia. *Becoming a Woman Who Walks with God.* Colorado Springs, CO: NavPress, 2004.

Kent, Carol. *Detours, Tow Trucks, and Angels in Disguise.* Colorado Springs, CO: NavPress, 1996. A collection of amusing anecdotes and heart-touching illustrations.

Larson, Craig Brian. *Contemporary Illustrations for Preachers, Teachers, and Writers.* Grand Rapids, MI: Baker, 1996. Filled with real-life stories about well-known athletes, novelists, and newsmakers.

McKenzie, E. C. *14,000 Quips & Quotes for Speakers, Writers, Editors, Preachers, and Teachers.* Grand Rapids, MI: Baker, 1990. All 14,000 entries are organized into 528 alphabetically listed subjects. Quotes range from the humorous to the reflective.

Rowell, Edward K., ed. *Quotes & Idea Starters for Preaching and Teaching.* Grand Rapids, MI: Baker, 2000. Topically arranged contemporary quotations from *Leadership Journal.*

General Resource Books for Speakers

Brown, Steve. *How to Talk So People Will Listen.* Grand Rapids, MI: Baker, 1999. Gives practical how-to's of effectively communicating to one person or a group.

Fast, Julius. *Body Language.* New York: M. Evans and Company, 2002. Teaches how to use body language and how to read the body language of others.

Griffin, Jack. *How to Say It Best.* Englewood Cliffs, NJ: Prentice Hall, 2005. A handbook for speakers on using facts, humor, visual aids, and body language.

Nash, Dr. Tom. *The Christian Communicator's Handbook.* Colorado Springs, CO: Victor, 1995. Integrates biblical principles with positive communication concepts.

Schloff, Laurie, and Marcia Yudkin. *Smart Speaking, Sixty-Second Strategies.* New York: Henry Holt and Co., 1996. A problem-solving guide to communicating effectively in a multitude of situations. Uniquely organized for quick reference. Offers practical advice for solving speech crises.

Proper Dress

Jackson, Carole. *Color Me Beautiful.* New York: Ballantine, 1980. The "textbook" on understandable color analysis, this book helps you learn how wearing colors that enhance your natural coloring will make you look healthier and more vibrant.

Molloy, John T. *Dress for Success.* New York: Warner, 1975. A secular approach on dressing for success, but includes important information on how men can look their best to enhance their message.

Specific Bible Study Resources

McBride, Neal. *How to Lead Small Groups.* Colorado Springs, CO: NavPress, 1990. A step-by-step guide to run an effective small group Bible study, fellowship, task, or support group. Includes practical exercises.

Nelson's Complete Book of Bible Maps and Charts. Nashville: Thomas Nelson, 1996. A visual survey and time lines of the entire Bible. Includes reproducible maps and charts.

Robinson, Haddon W. *Biblical Preaching*. Grand Rapids, MI: Baker, 2001. An extraordinary reference for anyone who teaches the Bible. Combines excellent how-to's for message development with a spiritual challenge for the speaker.

Sproul, R. C. *Knowing Scripture*. Downers Grove, IL: InterVarsity, 1978. Practical, concise, thorough—a readable guide for the serious student and/or teacher of the Bible. Excellent section on helpful tools for Bible study.

Strong, James. *The New Strong's Exhaustive Concordance of the Bible*. Nashville: Thomas Nelson, 1990, 2001. Enables the reader to locate any Scripture passage in the Bible.

Vine, W. E., Merrill F. Unger, and William White, Jr. *Vine's Complete Expository Dictionary of Old and New Testament Words*. Nashville: Thomas Nelson, 1985. The standard text for Bible students and teachers who desire accurate translations of Greek or Hebrew but have not studied the language themselves. A concordance, a dictionary, and a commentary all in one.

Wilkinson, Bruce, and Kenneth Boa. *Talk Thru the Bible*. Nashville: Thomas Nelson, 1983, 2005. A user-friendly reference tool to help you understand each book of the Bible, its historical context, and its place in Scripture.

Youngblood, Ronald F., gen. ed. *Nelson's New Illustrated Bible Dictionary*. Nashville: Thomas Nelson, 1995. Dependable findings and insights that will enrich study and teaching of the Bible.

Software Resources

Logos Bible Software—A full-service Bible software company that includes the Libronix Digital Library, containing hundreds of online Bible reference books, a parallel study Bible with your choice of translations, and passage studies, word studies, and topical studies available with a keystroke. This is my favorite reference tool. More information is available at www.logos.com.

General Resources for Bible Teaching

Bible Translations

Study different translations that reflect verbal and concept accuracy. Verbal accuracy follows the Greek or Hebrew text as closely as possible, and concept accuracy combines a fluid reading style with minimal verbal distortion. My favorites are the *New International Version*, the *New King James Version*, the *New American Standard Bible*, the *New Living Translation*, and the *King James Version*. For a refreshing, contemporary version of Scripture, read Eugene Peterson's *The Message*, along with your favorite translation.

Annotated Bible

Marginal notes, footnotes, and cross-referencing will save you a trip to a commentary or Bible dictionary with the helps offered in many study Bibles. Annotated Bibles should not take the place of other study helps, but they give a general overview of the meaning of a passage.

Commentary

Indispensable aid for understanding what the Bible means, a commentary provides a check-and-balance system for weighing your interpretation against a researched scholarly approach to the passage under consideration. There is a wide variety of commentaries available.

Concordance

This tool allows you to look up any key Bible word and have a listing of every place in Scripture where that word is used. It is an invaluable tool for finding the reference of a verse or for doing an in-depth word study. Concordances can be exhaustive or abbreviated and come in editions that match your preferred Bible translation.

Bible Dictionary

For descriptions of important Bible names, places, and key words, this resource is a handy reference for all Bible students. Many pictorial Bible dictionaries are on the market today.

Dictionary

A frequently overlooked reference is this most common of books. Use it often to compare general understanding of a key Bible word with the Hebrew or Greek meaning.

Thesaurus

A handy reference for enlarging your vocabulary and finding the words that most exactly express your ideas. This necessary tool will help with alliterative outlines.

Bible Atlas

The geography of a Bible story is much more understandable with the help of colorful maps of Bible lands. A good Bible atlas will give you a faster comprehension of events and places in the Scriptures. Check on the vast number of online helps that are available.

Internet Resources for Speakers

www.crosswalk.com—Click on "Bible Study Tools" for free access to:

Commentaries
Online Study Bible
Parallel Bible
Concordances
Dictionaries
Illustrations and more

www.gospelnet.com—Links to over 300 online Christian ministry sites, and many free speaker resource tools. Click on: Browse by "Interest" and Sort by "Content" for free access to:

Commentaries
Devotionals
Sermons and Sermon Aids
Bible Studies
Apologetics
Christian Literature
Streaming Media Resources, providing live & on-demand
        Internet media resources

www.BibleGateway.com—This site is linked to the homepage of www.gospelnet.com and key features include free access to:

Scripture "Passage Lookup" program
Scripture "Keyword Search"
Topical Index search option
Commentaries

www.nobs.org—The Network of Biblical Storytellers hosts story-telling events and festivals around the country and offers an online bookstore of resources specifically geared to biblical storytellers. Membership is inexpensive.

www.CarolKent.org—Click on: "Speak Up Seminars" for informa-tion on dates and locations for upcoming Original and Advanced Speak Up with Confidence seminars that are taught by Carol Kent and Speak Up staff members.

Author

CAROL KENT is a best-selling author and a popular international public speaker who is known for being hilariously funny, biblically sound, and heartbreakingly transparent in person and in print. She is a former radio show cohost and has often been a guest on *Focus on the Family* and a featured speaker at Women of Faith and Extraordinary Women events.

She is the president of Speak Up Speaker Services, a Christian speakers' bureau, and the founder and director of Speak Up with Confidence seminars, a ministry committed to helping Christians develop their communication skills. She has founded the nonprofit organization Speak Up for Hope, which benefits the families of incarcerated individuals.

She holds a master's degree in communication arts and a bachelor's degree in speech education. She has taught speech and drama and directed women's ministries at a large midwestern church. She serves on the advisory boards of the Advanced Writers and Speakers Association and MOPS International.

Her books include *When I Lay My Isaac Down, Becoming a Woman of Influence, Mothers Have Angel Wings, Secret Longings of the Heart, Tame Your Fears,* and *Detours, Tow Trucks, and Angels in Disguise* (all NavPress). She has also cowritten with Karen Lee-Thorp the *Designed for Influence* Bible studies (six books in the series, NavPress). Carol was the coauthor and general editor of the *Kisses of Sunshine* series of five books (Zondervan). She has also authored *A New Kind of Normal* (Thomas Nelson).

For more information, go to:
www.CarolKent.org ~ www.SpeakUpforHope.org ~
www.SpeakUpSpeakerServices.com

CHECK OUT THESE OTHER GREAT TITLES FROM CAROL KENT!

 ### Secret Longings of the Heart
978-1-57683-360-5

Daringly honest, powerfully encouraging, and thoroughly biblical, this book will help you explore your longings for fulfillment as well as help you deal with disappointment when longings go unfulfilled.

Tame Your Fears
978-1-57683-359-9

If you've grown tired of being victimized by fear, let Carol Kent show you how God desires to tame your fears and help you move toward a more productive and satisfying future.

 ### Becoming a Woman of Influence
978-1-57683-933-1

Do you seek deep, connective relationships that will encourage you to grow? Discover principles for building solid relationships through simple steps to mentoring. Learn to impact others Jesus' way.

When I Lay My Isaac Down
978-1-57683-474-9

Coping with her son's arrest and trial for first-degree murder, Carol Kent opens her heart to share priceless lessons on choosing hope over despair.

To order copies, call NavPress at 1-800-366-7788 or log on to www.navpress.com.

NAVPRESS